ELECTRONIC WORKSHOP

TYPOGRAPHY

RotoVision

TYPOGRAPHY

YOLANDA ZAPPATERRA

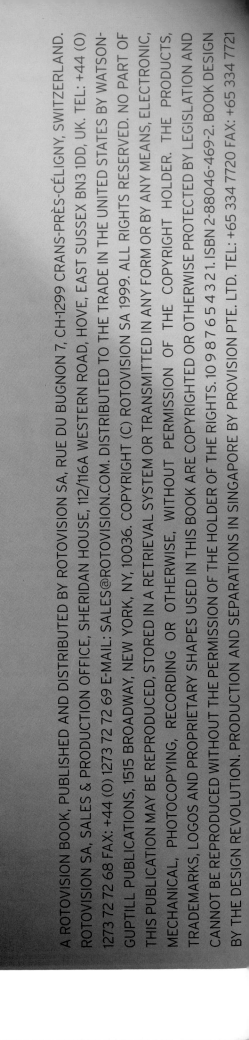

Carmelo Gómez

UNDERGROUND RESCUE

Hkj01236H

BANDWIDTH

Eban

Horizontales plus ouvertes

Graisses corrigées

CANDY

nothingness. Existing where there is nothing is the meaning of the phrase, "Form is emptiness." That all things are provided for by nothingness is the meaning of the phrase, "Emptiness is form." One should not think

frieze
INTERNATIONAL ART MAGAZINE

print out of me enough w/ wha... (re-drawn by hand)

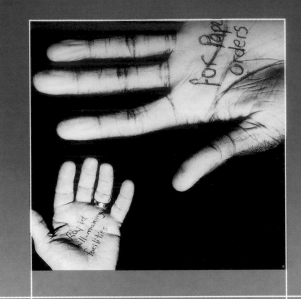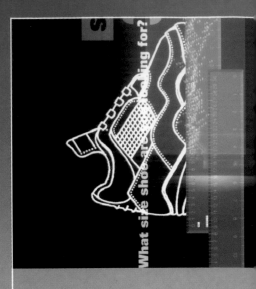

Absolutely no one, when you tell them you're working on a book about graphic design or illustration, says, 'What's that then?' Small children understand illustration and its relationship with design, text and narrative. But tell well-seasoned designers that you're working on a book about typography, and they'll guardedly respond with 'so how are you defining typography?' Many of them, on being asked if they'd like to put forward a project for inclusion in the book, responded with 'but I don't originate type. I'm not a type designer.' To answer the thorny definition question – and indeed to define the parameters of the book – I decided that *Electronic Workshop: Typography* would look at graphics jobs in which the type was originated for the project, or in which type was used in a particularly effective way. It was a necessarily broad definition, and obviously one which afforded a wide range of work from which to choose contributors. It sat within the parameters of the *Oxford English Dictionary*'s definition of typography as the arrangement and appearance of printed matter – but updated it to include the design arrangement of film matter, printed metal, websites, exhibition hoardings, TV screen idents, signage; the arrangement and appearance of the stuff that surrounds us, as *Wallpaper** magazine might say.

The next thing to decide was how the
book would look at those arrangements
and type's role within them. Rather :han
lecture readers on the history of type and
how to use it – there are many very good
books out there that do that – it would,
through 15 international real-life projects
ranging from transport signage systems
and Pacific Rim websites to European
station idents and American exhibit ons,
look at the use of digital type and cover
the effect of the computer on type and
typography. Just 15 years ago, type and
image on a newspaper, brochure, poster,
book etc. were, for the most part,
mutually exclusive. The two firmly
occupied their own spaces, often nicely
juxtaposed but rarely occupying the
same space. Now that's changed; type
and imagery can offer an integrated
and seamless graphic solution, largely
due to the cost benefits of new
technology. Do the maths: pre-scanner,
pre-Photoshop, pre-DTP, the labour costs
of technicians, typographers and repro

house staff all spending hours stripping in type over a photo or illustration, or masking that type into an image, were prohibitively expensive for most publishers and clients. And the error of margin was so high that often the finished product wasn't worth the expense anyway. But the computer changed all that, enabling designers to realise those ideas which had previously been so prohibitively expensive. In doing so – and coinciding with a growing reliance on the image – the computer also changed the very nature of design; now, instead of pictures being used to enliven pages or make text more palatable, they began to replace the text altogether, or even become the text! Jonathan Barnbrook's design for the Damien Hirst book, *I WANT TO SPEND THE REST OF MY LIFE EVERYWHERE, WITH EVERYONE, ONE TO ONE, ALWAYS, FOREVER, NOW.*, illustrates this idea of text as image; it's difficult to tell where the book's design stops and the art and analysis start, a symbiotic relationship is created. Martin Venezky's *Bordertown*, a book of photography and writings by David Perry and Barry Gifford, offers an equally well-balanced project, and both are fine examples of what can be achieved with some fantastic creative solutions and a few software programs.

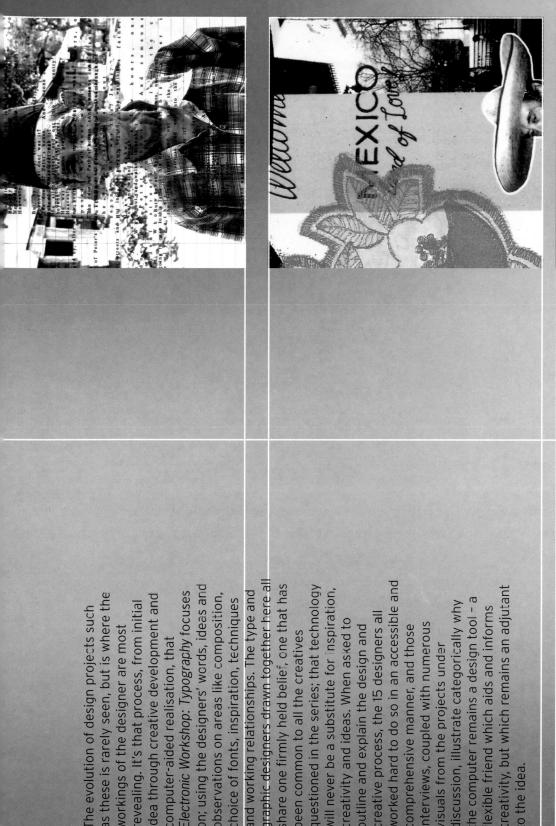

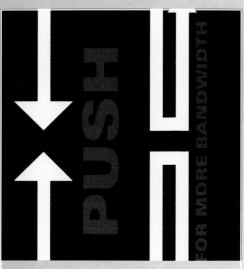

The evolution of design projects such as these is rarely seen, but is where the workings of the designer are most revealing. It's that process, from initial idea through creative development and computer-aided realisation, that *Electronic Workshop: Typography* focuses on; using the designers' words, ideas and observations on areas like composition, choice of fonts, inspiration, techniques and working relationships. The type and graphic designers drawn together here all share one firmly held belief, one that has been common to all the creatives questioned in the series; that technology will never be a substitute for inspiration, creativity and ideas. When asked to outline and explain the design and creative process, the 15 designers all worked hard to do so in an accessible and comprehensive manner, and those interviews, coupled with numerous visuals from the projects under discussion, illustrate categorically why the computer remains a design tool – a flexible friend which aids and informs creativity, but which remains an adjutant to the idea.

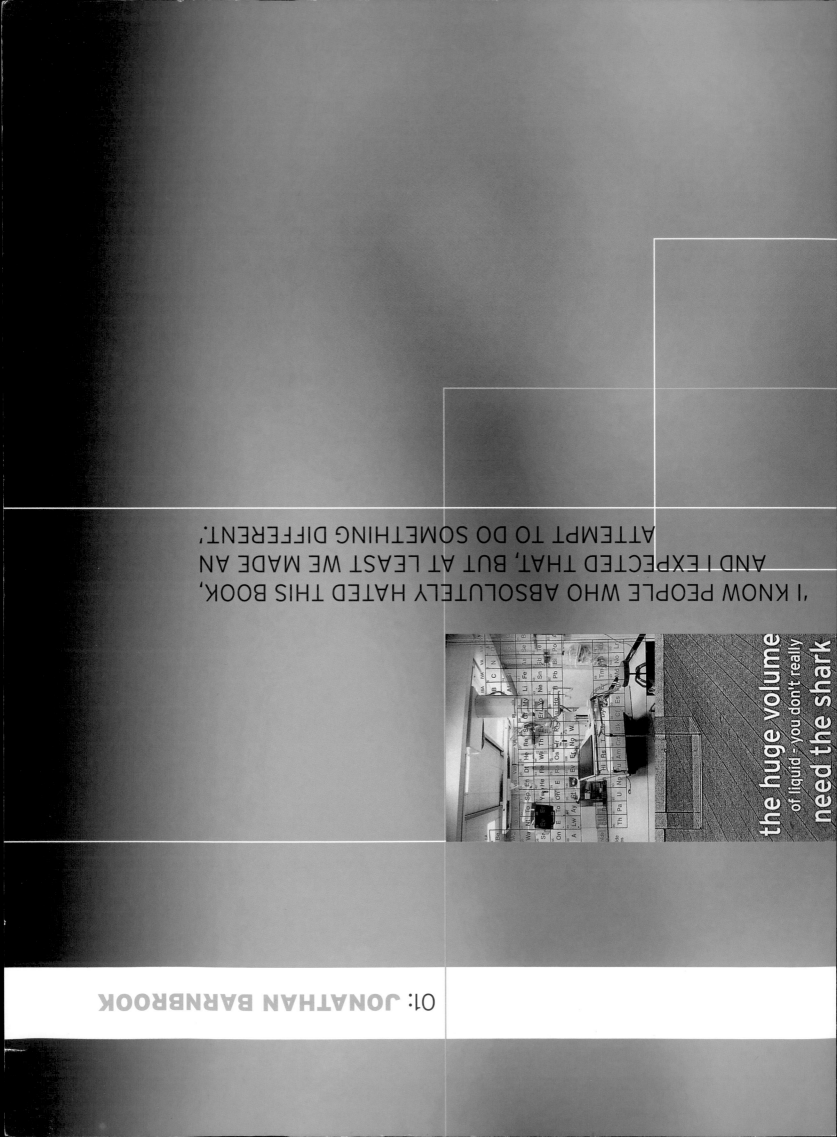

'I KNOW PEOPLE WHO ABSOLUTELY HATED THIS BOOK, AND I EXPECTED THAT, BUT AT LEAST WE MADE AN ATTEMPT TO DO SOMETHING DIFFERENT.'

the huge volume
of liquid - you don't really
need the shark

Biography

Jonathan Barnbrook was off to speak at a conference in Brazil when I first caught up with him, which gives an indication of the stature of this quietly spoken and thoughtful 33-year-old British type designer, turned designer, turned top ad man with global clients such as Guinness and Nike. Barnbrook studied at London colleges St Martins and the Royal College of Art from 1985–1992, (after a two year diploma in graphics and a year of higher diploma 'because I couldn't get on a degree course', he says!) and since that time has worked as an independent graphic designer, eschewing the 'let's-get-big-and-run-a-consultancy' business model for a small one-man studio in Soho. He does own his own type company and an expectedly idiosyncratic website, virus, through which he sells some of his fonts, and a couple of years ago he became more involved in moving image typography and live-action directing.

It was Barnbrook's live action work that led to an 18-month collaboration with artist Damien Hirst, the result of which was the book *I WANT TO SPEND THE REST OF MY LIFE EVERYWHERE, WITH EVERYONE, ONE TO ONE, ALWAYS, FOREVER, NOW,* for Booth-Clibborn Editions. The book is monumental in size, scope and ideas, and it does things never attempted before in print – which is why Barnbrook took the job: 'We thought seriously about the role of art books and the content and design of previous ones, and from the start decided it was important that it wasn't a boring art book that sits on library shelves and gets dusty. Damien comes from a popular culture background and he wanted the book to reflect that, and I wouldn't have done it if it was just big pictures in a book,' he says.

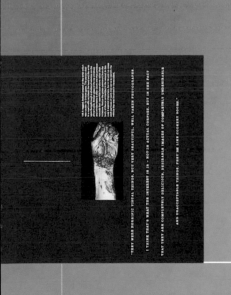

Background and initial approach

'Damien had quite strong ideas about what he wanted the book to look like, and say and do, but he wasn't fascistic about it, I think he was one of the most open-minded artists I've worked with,' says Barnbrook. He believes that whereas other artists working in one medium might mistakenly think they can do another well, Damien recognises his limitations:

'Because he works in a similar way to designers, in that often he doesn't paint the paintings himself or make the sculptures himself, but has the central idea and commissions a specialist to realise it, I think there's a bit more respect there for the graphic designer,' explains Barnbrook.

As their starting point, the two began by thinking about the atmosphere around the work. They let ideas and the book itself develop organically, rather than through a strictly flat-planned linear approach. Barnbrook says he was 'aiming for a graphic treatment that would successfully enhance the concepts being expressed in Damien's work, rather than obscure the work. While it was all pre-existing work, the point of a book is that you can't recreate the reality, you're dealing with pages, not three-dimensional space, so you have to work in time with those pages, not just show shots of the work.' While it would be impossible to look at the book's whole here, a number of the ideas and techniques for this transferral are detailed below.

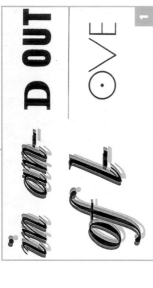

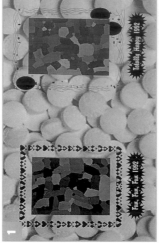

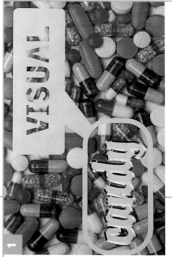

1 'It's important for me to be able to see the whole picture absolutely, and so most of my creative process is done on computer, visualising ideas through scanning, outputting and refining,' says Barnbrook.

2 A very early section of the book shows an early installation by Hirst, and its positioning was a reaction against the way most art books are designed and seen as coffee table books: 'People browsing through it at somebody's house would come across these really nasty pictures; of someone who's blown his head off, had their wrists cut in a fatal car crash', says Barnbrook.

3 The style of Hirst's name relates to the medical theme carried throughout the book and Hirst's work, but also represents Hirst as product: 'He's reached a level of fame where he projects an image in the media and that media's taken over his persona to create a new dynamic. I was trying to represent Hirst as maybe an inhuman corporation', says Barnbrook.

4 'I based this layout on cigarette packaging, because the actual point of this work is that the cigarette butts represent existential human beings – it's ridiculous to talk about cigarette butts like that, but the titles are Died Out, Explored and Died Out, Examined.'

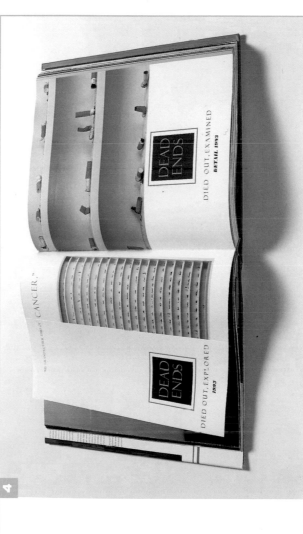

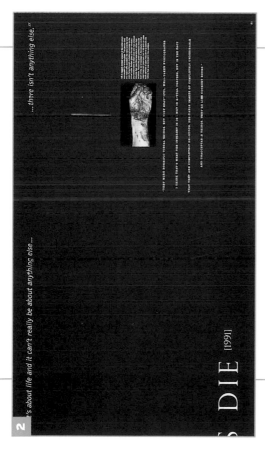

'A LOT OF PEOPLE THINK THE POP-UPS IN THE BOOK BELITTLE THE WORK, BUT PICASSO SAID THAT TO BE A GOOD ARTIST YOU HAVE TO LEARN TO PAINT LIKE A CHILD, AND I THINK TO APPRECIATE ART YOU HAVE TO BE AS PLAYFUL AS A CHILD, BECAUSE ART IS SUPPOSED TO BE PLAYFUL, IT'S SUPPOSED TO HAVE A LIVELY ASPECT.'

Design and interpretation

One area both artists felt strongly about was text: 'Because we wanted to respond to the contemporary world (rather than legitimise art, which a lot of those books do),' says Barnbrook, 'the book does away with lengthy academic essays, using very little text. Aside from an essay at the beginning of the book and some smaller ones dotted throughout the book, a chapter incorporating news cuttings, letters, newspaper cartoons and so on offers the only comment on Damien's work.' He does admit that with hindsight he thinks the book suffers from a lack of criticism: 'Even if people didn't read it, it ought to be there in addition to the other pieces, for some sort of balance.'

5 'I'm trying to project Damien's work in the typography, and although there's no direct explanation, this was trying to relate to the title, Mother and Child Divided, which is about separation and birth. I also designed it like this because the piece appeared in the Venice Biennial next to a very famous church with a Madonna and Child. It's a reference which I hope people get.'

Illustrating the way all big art deals with mortality, the book opens with black pages and closes with white; 'because it's all about waiting to die and existence,' explains Barnbrook. So the black through to white represents 'an accident or tragedy which ends in a hospital, also reflected in the interior of the ambulance and the last image, a hospital corridor,' he adds.

Hirst's obsession with medical imagery gave Barnbrook the opportunity to reference things like medical charts and stock photography, images which are innocuous in themselves but taken in the context of the book acquire more sinister tones. 'It was important that we didn't take the pictures ourselves because the stock photography reveals social structures,' says Barnbrook.

Because most art books try to talk about social context of an artist and their work but usually fail to express or show that context, there's a very particular attempt in this book to do that. 'Again it's trying to relate the work to real life... when people see art they don't see any relation to what's going on, it makes no connection with other areas of their lives, like walking down a street or reading a newspaper, and we wanted to address that,' says Barnbrook.

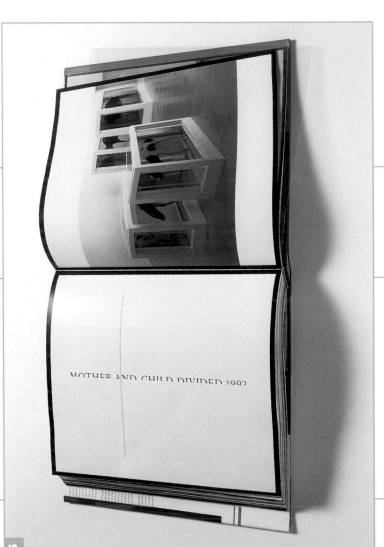

MOTHER AND CHILD DIVIDED 1993

They did so in a section which opens with pictures Damien did when he was a child; 'not the typically charming child pictures one sees, because they're kind of rubbish, but they're about not taking oneself too seriously,' explains Barnbrook. From these naïve paintings the chapter moves into references which put Damien's work firmly in the real world; cartoons, press cuttings, letters and the like, 'all of which show that an artist actually had an effect on society, his work was in common currency,' says Barnbrook. 'It all gives a bigger picture of what an artist is. I don't know many people who actually read art books, because the text is separated from the image – people tend to look at the images and just read the captions. So incorporating these comments from the press – which are all some form of critical comment on a piece of work in popular culture – I think helps the understanding of the work,' he adds.

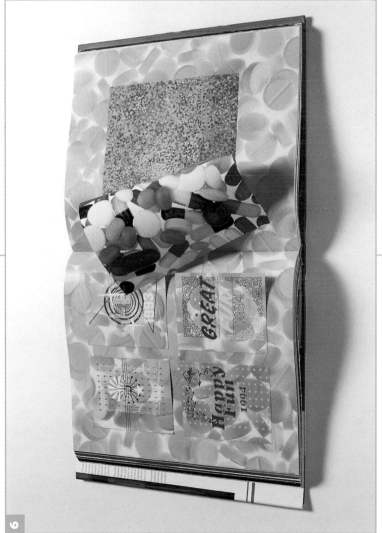

'YOU HAVE TO HAVE THE IDEA BEFORE YOU CAN GO TO THE COMPUTER OR YOUR WORK WILL LACK AUTHORITY. THE WAY I DO THAT IS WITH A PENCIL, PAPER AND STUPID LITTLE DRAWINGS.'

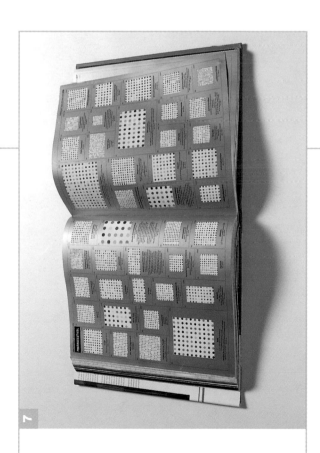

6 Barnbrook says these relate to greetings cards graphics and the artificial optimism of the titles, like the artificial optimism of Happy Birthday cards, so he used 'the worst kind of graphics and the worst kind of type'.

7 The type on the spot paintings is copied directly from a medical catalogue. The spot paintings are named after drug compounds, under which is reproduced the correct drug information, lifted from the catalogue, and the dimensions of the painting.

Computers

'I find the best way to begin is to have the ideas and then go to the computer and try to visualise them, through scanning, outputting and refining. After all, most design is a process of refining. It's important for me to be able to see the whole picture absolutely, and so most of my creative process is done on computer. Having said that, while you play around with the images you've scanned in, you've got to have had the idea first, you can't just go to the computer and hope that it will just happen, you need a rough or gut feeling. Some people will use the defaults whether they have a Photoshop filter or a letter press, but you have to have the brain to use it. There has always been good work and bad work, I don't think the Mac has been the cause of that, it's always there.'

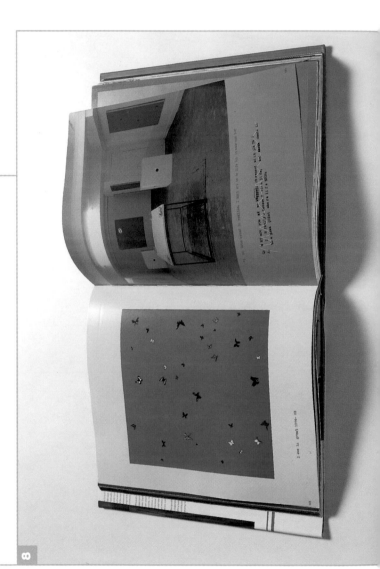

8 For 'In And Out Of Love', paintings created by butterflies hatching and sticking to the wet canvasses as they flew around the gallery, the type was created using an old Remette typewriter which sits proudly in Barnbrook's studio. 'The keys and type mimic the rhythm of butterflies. The tapping and mistakes are part of that, and too the fluttering of fingers over the keys brings to mind butterfly wings.'

Working process and problems

Through the whole process, Hirst, Barnbrook and American editor Robert Violette would put forward ideas. 'For example, in the first few pages, the use of captions without actual pictures, which is a very graphic design idea, was Damien's,' says Barnbrook. 'The important thing is to have confidence in people working on the project, which may sound stupid, but to believe that the designer knows what he's doing and so on. You can't have everything worked out, and that's why there are so many boring book designs, because people aren't prepared to take a chance,' complains Barnbrook.

When the book came to being printed in Hong Kong, Hirst and Barnbrook had to spend three weeks sorting out the myriad technical problems inevitable in such an ambitious project. Acetate sheets, holes punched in pages, spinning discs, pop-ups and elaborate three-dimensional paper engineering had never been done before in one book, and many of the elements had never been attempted before at all. 'For example, pop-ups only work properly if you can get the book to lie absolutely flat, which is impossible in such a big book, so we had to find a way around that and use very simple mechanisms. Similarly, with the spot picture there's a hole punched into each page which has to be in a slightly different position on each page, because the pages don't align 100%,' says Barnbrook.

9 'This was a letter sent to Damien, in which a razor blade was hidden in the envelope, and the postmark says "Send a little happiness, post a card at Easter, and the two taken together strongly brought to my mind the wounded Christ on the Cross,' explains Barnbrook.

10 'Art in the 1990s is so much more knowing than '70s' art, more ironic. It metaphorically places things in quotation marks much more than we did 20 or even ten years ago. Similarly, graphic design is a language which contains elements and signs that are significant social symbols. A script face isn't necessarily "real" when you use it, referring to all those kinds of romantic script faces and associated vocabulary. So here, with something called "The Lovers", you expect something quite romantic. It makes you think of Rodin's sculpture "The Lovers", which is seen as romantic, but the words are in direct contrast to the actual pieces of work shown in the fold-out spread, so the context of the typeface changes. What's inside the spread is actually about death, the idea of the sensation and emotion. The script then takes on a different context, it looks nasty, not pleasant. It's a cynical use of the face,' explains Barnbrook.

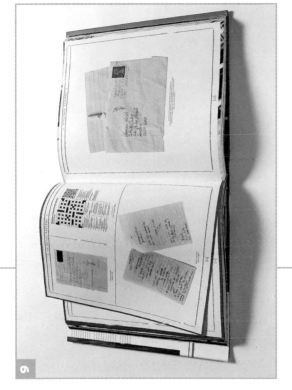

9

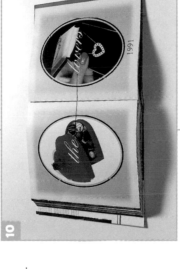

10

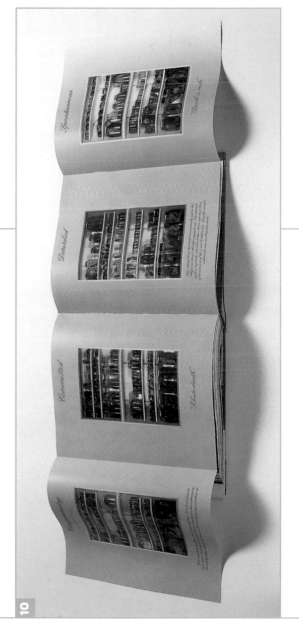

10

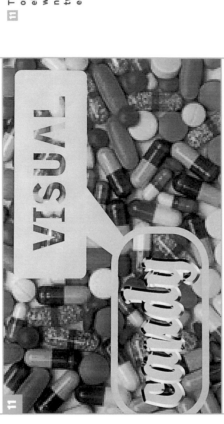

11 The book developed organically but once elements of different pages were in place, spreads did not change much as these two versions – the top an early one – illustrate.

'I know people who absolutely hated this book, and I expected that, but at least we made an attempt to do something different. The project was really poorly paid for the amount of time spent on it, but I think as a graphic designer you get very few chances to do something really different. You can do something that looks different, but to do something intellectually different is quite difficult.'

'There's a lot that's gone on in typographic design that hasn't been taken on by the fine art world, and if you believe that graphic messages aren't transparent and that they have the possibility to enhance the work they're representing, then you should do work like this, rather than just go back to the classic layout. This project was a nightmare, but in the end the reason I did it was because the possibility of doing it was far more exciting than not doing it,' says Barnbrook simply.

'GRAPHIC DESIGN IS A LANGUAGE WHICH CONTAINS ELEMENTS AND SIGNS THAT ARE SIGNIFICANT SOCIAL SYMBOLS. A SCRIPT FACE ISN'T NECESSARILY REAL WHEN YOU USE IT, REFERRING TO ALL THOSE KINDS OF ROMANTIC SCRIPT FACES AND ASSOCIATED VOCABULARY.'

12 Throughout the book I used
sanserif pre-existing fonts
and one of mine, Delux. One
font I used, DIN, was
designed by committee in
Germany to be a standard,
clear typeface, which
additionally creates an
emotional distance,' says
Barnbrook.

HARDWARE/SOFTWARE
G3 300 Mhz Mac.
QuarkXpress, Freehand, Fontographer, Photoshop.

DETAILS
Jonathan Barnbrook
Studio 12
10 Archer Street
London W1 7HG
UK
tel: +44 171 287 3848

Biography

The Netherlands has already developed a reputation for leading the way in the policy debate in the field of new media culture in Europe, and one of the leading players in the debate is Mieke Gerritzen. The 37-year-old Dutch designer may not have the clout of mega-designers like Lambie Nairn or Fitch, or the kudos of web houses like Antirom or Online Magic, the instant trendiness of Tomato or the Attik, but this thoughtful print and web designer and new media lecturer at the Rietveld Academie has been involved in a number of projects which have garnered praise and awards from all the right quarters, including prizes for her print work in books, catalogues and posters, a permanent collection at the San Francisco Museum of Modern Art and receipt of the prestigious Rotterdam Design Prize in 1997 for her Leestafel (Reading Table) for the Society for Old and new Media.

'The Society for Old and New Media, founded two years ago, is in the Waag, a building that once formed part of the medieval gate of the city of Amsterdam. Its role is to draw attention to the radical changes in new media and in the exchange of information in general. It also draws attention to the fact that these changes are often determined by financial and technological limits. Its main concern is the question of how an informed society can develop amid the tools of the information society. Its research approach simultaneously employs reflection, participation, creation and presentation. This is the basis of the Society's work,' explains Gerritzen.

'RIGHT NOW, WE (DESIGNERS) ARE TOTALLY DEPENDENT
ON THE TECHNICIANS WHO ARE DEVELOPING OUR
DESIGNERS' TOOLS. I THINK THAT DESIGNERS SHOULD
ASK MORE FOR THEIR NEEDS INSTEAD OF WAITING
UNTIL SOMETHING NEW COMES OUT.'

PUSH FOR MORE BANDWIDTH

1

THE SOCIETY FOR
MORE AND MORE
MEDIA AT HYBRID WORKSPACE
DOCUMENTA X
KASSEL, GERMANY

FROM 8 T/M 17 JULY 1997
WE WILL SPEED YOU UP TO ESCAPE VELOCITY

MORE

8 juli
2400 bps flintstone speed

9 juli

10 juli
9600 bps obsolete

DE WAAG   MAATSCHAPPIJ   PROJEKTEN   HISTORIE   RESTAURANTCAFE   ARCHIEF   ENGLISH

1   'We Want More Bandwidth',
a virtual pressure group
initiated by De Waag for
Documenta X in Kassel in
1997, illustrates Gerritzen's
campaigning style of work
and shares that style with
the Hybrid Project, which
came out of the same event.
Realistic photographs
convinced people – and
newspapers such as The
Herald Tribune – that the
campaign was real.

1

PUSH
DEMAND BANDWIDTH
BACK

Background

The ground floor of the Waag building is a café
and restaurant, styled in keeping with the
medieval character of the building, and the fact
that most Dutch cafés have a reading table
with newspapers and books formed the basic
idea of the Reading Table for Old and New
Media. The electronic table has eight places:
four for new media, internet surfing and
e-mail, and four old media places for
newspapers and books. It's a hybrid product
that combines many design disciplines. 'The
relationship between old and new was a pivotal
consideration for the design of both the
physical table itself, and its digital interfaces,'
says Gerritzen.

1

BANDWIDTH

'FOR THE ARTISTS AND DESIGNERS WHO WORK WITH TECHNOLOGY, NO AMOUNT OF
TALENT, NO GROUND-BREAKING AESTHETIC, NO ASTONISHING INSIGHT MAKES UP FOR
THE INABILITY TO DEMONSTRATE THEIR WORK ON A COMPUTER IN REAL TIME IN
FRONT OF AN AUDIENCE.' PETER LUNENFELD

'New media didn't only facilitate the successful combination of various disciplines within the virtual environment of the screen: they also became a part of the physical product. The guiding principle in the design of the table was the creation of atmosphere and ambience. The interface is devoid of the designs of the software industry. One no longer sees known computer programs. The reader no longer looks through the glasses of an American software company, when in contact with Taiwan, Paris, New York or their neighbour. One uses the local design to look at and communicate with the rest of the world,' says Gerritzen. 'The Society backed the development of this kind of reading table browser, and the concept can be extended to other locations,' she adds.

Initial approach and development

Two years on and Gerritzen has completed another project for the Society, called The Hybrid Media Lounge, which continues her campaigning work started two years ago on Bandwidth, a project which came out of the Hybrid Workspace Project curated by media theorist and networker Geert Lovink during the Documenta X exhibition in Kassel in 1997. 'I have special interests in campaigning styles, in the sense of mergendizing my own work; the way I can "copy and paste" the same things and place them in another context. The Bandwidth campaign was a good example of that. This campaign was only virtual, but people thought it was real, because they saw these very realistic pictures. For example The Herald Tribune published a picture with the caption: "European advocates billboarding the demand for better Net service." But this picture was fake. And that's the discussion about media in general, virtual or real, what can you believe or not, and whether it matters,' says Gerritzen.

For the Hybrid site, Gerritzen and project initiator Geert Lovink spent some six months discussing and developing the concept and meaning of the project before they started. 'Developing the project in the Society For Old and New Media meant we were working with many designers and software developers. We always put together a team for a project, because new media is inherent to working together, and you can never have the necessary knowledge about all the different aspects that you need by yourself,' explains Gerritzen.

The Hybrid Media Lounge website consists of a database and the archived material of the Hybrid Workspace from the Documenta X festival which, in Gerritzen's words, 'begins the visual mapping of electronically driven cultural networking in Europe. It's a collection of Cultural European Media Institutes, all of whom are working on their mission and developing software and strategies. Not one of these institutes is ready, and that's the reason for the look and feel of this website: under construction! It's an attempt to begin two ambitious projects: building a directory of hybrid art-political-

2

2 The introduction page to the Hybrid Media Lounge database shows an animated gif, depicting a man digging in what seems to be a heap of sand, but is actually the map of Europe. The database is entered by clicking on the 'OK' button and can be searched in four areas: Hard Data, Soft Data, Context and Network. In the fifth area is archived material from the Hybrid Workspace.

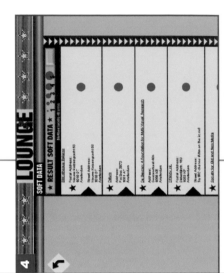

3 In Soft Data you can search through members' 'ratings' of themselves in terms of several qualities, topics and emphases, by using the pull-down menus, and you can see how these ratings are distributed across a map of Europe. You can use the navigation to move the map of Europe to the left or to the right, or to zoom into a specific area or country. When you click on one of the red dots, you go to a list of organisations and their ratings.

4 This page shows a list of organisations as a result of the 'Soft Data' interface.

cultural-digital activities in Europe and visually mapping the networks between their instigators. The meaning of this site is that it will grow, it's a network which will never be finished.'

The website database is also represented on a CD-ROM, which will be distributed with other media, for example in the UK with *MUTE* magazine. 'We decided to create the CD-ROM, which actually is only a freeze of the website, because not all the institutes involved have very good online capabilities,' says Gerritzen. 'It also enables an overview of the growth aspect of this field. We will make a freeze every year, as an archive and also to get an idea of the changing aspects in design during the coming years,' she adds.

While the site acts as a database for Europe's emergent new media organisations, it and a related book, *New Media Culture in Europe*, combine to work together in raising questions about the role of cultural organisations in the development of this growing field. 'These organisations are working as research centres, developing applications of new media for the public domain, investigating new ways of learning and communicating. In the process they are breaking down traditional barriers between arts disciplines and between arts and science, commercial and not-for-profit, producer and consumer,' says the book's production co-ordinator, Julia van Mourik.

Gerritzen's 'Under construction' site enabled her to use the bold graphics and typography she favours: 'I like the pamphlet-style; political typography. Most of the things I work for are related to media critics and politic statements in the cultural world. The way I use the typography became recognisable for these things. But I don't want to do this all my life, I think about changing to very thin small fonts in the future,' she says. And she doesn't share the fears some designers have about using type online: 'Lots of designers don't like the web because of the typographical limits. I don't mind, I try to get the same style by playing with those limitations,' she asserts. For the site - with its yellow colour and the 'under construction' look as the basic design idea - she chose Helvetica Condensed Extra Black, 'because most of the time I use the same font types.' She also chose it because its strong, political and warning-sign connotations suit the design.

5 In 'Hard Data' you can search via members' names, languages, home countries and websites.

6 Network1 offers another search mechanism, as it covers the relationships between members (as described by them). You can also read members' own definitions of the word 'network'. You start by selecting an organisation in the upper pull-down menu. When you move your mouse over the little yellow squares under the subjects (in this example 'Familiarity'), the name of a related organisation appears in the white text field at the bottom of the interface. If you click 'View', the name of the organisation which was in the text field below moves up to the pull-down menu. When you click 'Go' you will go to a detailed description of this organisation. The text field below will now show an organisation which is 'Familiar' to this one.

Clicking on the 'Go there' button in the Network1 interface takes you to NETWORK2, which contains a detailed description of the organisation's structure, its topics, location etc. It also has a sub-menu which allows you to view additional data such as events, projects, network and value.

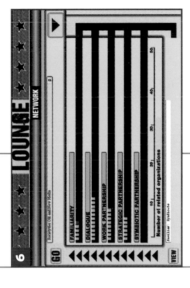

7 In 'Context' you can see what kind of resources – hardware, bandwidth, cash and flesh – members have to work with country by country and search by that information. By clicking on the name of the country of your choice, you go to a list of media organisations that are located in that country.

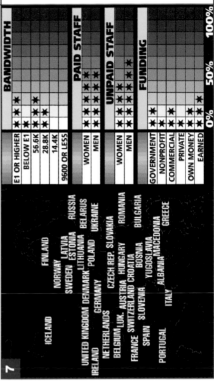

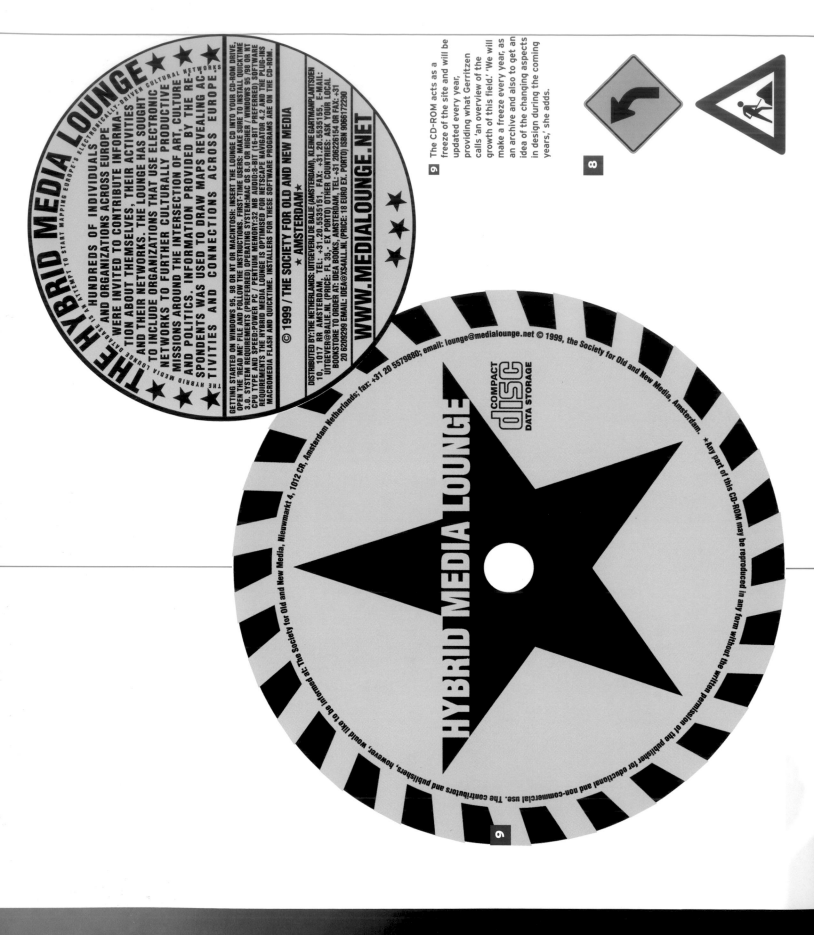

9 The CD-ROM acts as a freeze of the site and will be updated every year, providing what Gerritzen calls 'an overview of the growth of this field.' 'We will make a freeze every year, as an archive and also to get an idea of the changing aspects in design during the coming years,' she adds.

8

Designing for the web

While many design commentators and practitioners complain about the over-design of websites, in terms of their usability, navigation, content, structure etc., Gerritzen believes that the term 'over-design' is a matter of design mentality or language. 'In the beginning of the new media period came the whole group of Photoshop designers. The more layers, the more blurry was the work. I think it's more important to develop a style and use the growing technical possibilities in a functional way. In the case of my work, I always try to find simple and logical systems in form and navigation. But sometimes even my basic ideas are not easy to realise,' she says. She thinks the situation will only improve when designers wrest control from technicians: 'Digital media emerged from technology and are developed by technicians, who of necessity created their first visual designs. Designers – some for quite some time – have been working to improve this by exploring the significance of the visual power of the medium, but the majority of designers aren't interested at all, because they find the medium too limited. They'd rather wait until the medium is improved and the experimental stage is over with. But it is precisely in this experimental stage that the creativity of designers is important. In principle, this has little to do with technical complexity. We think more quickly than technology develops. The conceptual space of ideas grows more quickly than cyberspace. Designers can get the jump on technology and try to make their creative ideas influence its development. And when we've left the grey, technical period behind, a new world will open to us,' she concludes.

'IN DESIGNING NEW FORMS OF COMMUNICATION, WE MUST COHERENTLY COMBINE VERY DIFFERENT DISCIPLINES. THE CONTEXT OF THE DESIGN IS ALSO INCREASING IN IMPORTANCE. THE WORLD WIDE WEB IS SO LARGE, SO INTERNATIONAL AND DIFFICULT TO GAIN AN OVERVIEW OF, THAT IT WINDS UP SEEMING BLAND AND FACELESS. THIS IS WHY IDENTITY, IMAGE AND ENVIRONMENT ARE INCREASING IN IMPORTANCE.'

8 Stock art road signs are used as part of the site's design, which is based on the 'under construction' theme, 'because the current European landscape of art, technology and media institutions are in an under construction stage. The typography and use of icons borrow their inspiration from this theme,' explains Gerritzen.

10 The navigation bar features this icon man running up and down. Clicking on him activates the soundtrack.

DETAILS

Mieke Gerritzen
Society for Old and New Media
Nieuwmarkt 4
1023 CR Amsterdam
The Netherlands
tel: + 3 12 0557 9898
fax: + 3 12 0557 9880
e-mail: mieke@vpro.nl

CREDITS

www.medialounge.net
Producer: Philippe Taminiau
Editors: Laura Martz, Geert Lovink, Thorsten Schilling and Marleen Stikker
Design co-ordinator: Mieke Gerritzen
Database co-ordinator: Bente Van Bourgondien
Designers: Jan Enning, Sonja Radenkovic and Janine Huizenga

HARDWARE/SOFTWARE
Javascript, Flash, php, mysql, Photoshop.

'THE PRINCIPAL QUALITY OF PARISINE IS ITS ROUND, HUMAN, FRIENDLY ATMOSPHERE. THIS IS VERY IMPORTANT FOR SIGNAGE IN BAD CONDITIONS: WE USE THE METRO TO GO TO WORK, WE ARE LATE BECAUSE OF THE METRO, BUT WE'RE ALL IN THE SAME BOAT!'

Graisses corrigées

Contre-formes différenciées

Biography

After having been trained at the Atelier Nationale de Recherche Typographique (anrt), Jean-François Porchez (born 1964) worked as a typeface designer & consultant at Dragon Rouge. His two first type designs, ff Angie (89–95) & Apolline (93–95), were prize-winning entries at the international Morisawa typeface competitions. By 1994, he had created the new typeface for Le Monde. In 1996, he created Parisine, intended for the signages of the Paris Métro, & Anisette, with reference to the French poster designers of the 1930s.

Today, through Porchez Typofonderie, he designs custom typefaces for companies such as RATP (Public transport in Paris), Automobiles Peugeot, Costa Crocieres, Sita, and distributes his retails typefaces.

He regulary gives conferences, teaches typography and type design at École nationale supérieure des arts décoratifs (ensad) in Paris. He is a member of the Typographic Circle & the Association typographique internationale (ATypI), for which he is the French representative & board member. He contributes regulary to international graphic publications & published Lettres Françaises, and books (in French & English) that show all the contemporary French digital typefaces.

He was awarded the Prix Charles Peignot in 1998 in recognition of his outstanding contributions in the areas of type design & typography and to the typographic community.

Parisine

Background and Brief

In 1996 Jean-François Porchez was invited to create a new typeface and corporate identity for Paris's transport system RATP, comprising the Paris Métro, suburban RER lines and city bus lines. The existing display typefaces for RATP (Régie Autonome des Transports Parisiens) were a disparate mishmash of faces which had joined the RATP font palette over years, including Frutiger faces created almost 30 years earlier, a custom font for RER designed by Albert Boton and versions of Helvetica and Gill Sans. 'RATP asked the big distributors, including Linotype and Agfa France, for a specific Helvetica, condensed by ten per cent, as it was one of the faces already being used by the company for their city bus line corporate signage system. But because you can't purchase a font, only its rights of use, Helvetica is in fact a bad choice; it exists in too many different versions, and there was the

danger of ending up with contrasting signage. Also, RATP needed to be able to control the fonts being used by subcontractors who work for them to create a uniform style,' says Porchez.

'I was brought in by Martine Turner from Agfa France who thought that a local, more personal solution would be better. Meeting with her and RATP, I decided to come along with creative answers rather than the prices, commercial and technical answers; I proposed a new typeface based on Helvetica in width but more open and rounded to keep the legibility in narrower versions,' he adds.

1 This typeface, Le Monde Sans, was completed for *Le Monde* newspaper in 1996 and led Porchez to believe that 'contrasts and open counters are crucial'. It had a direct bearing on the design of Parisine.

2 For his starting point, Porchez was asked to base Parisine on Helvetica. He designed wider terminals on the a, f and t, along with the capital letters and figures. The caps are also shorter than the ascenders to help word shape recognition. Studies on legibility prove that our eyes 'read' the top third of the x-height, so with contrasted terminals and more emphasis on certain letters and accents, Porchez believes that Parisine is more legible than Helvetica.

Helvetica
Helvetica
Helvetica
Helvetica

Parisine
Parisine
Parisine
Parisine

2

Parisine

Eha

Chasse capitale

Montant plus ouverte

Horizontale plus aplatie

Sortie affinée

Œil plus grand

Place d'Italie

Bobigny 683

©1996, Jean-François Porchez, Porchez Typofonderie

Parisine (en noir) comparé à l'Helvetica (en blanc)

PORCHEZ Typofonderie

1

L'Monde Sans est la version linéale-déclinaison des versions à empattements. Comme le faisait auparavant l'italique, ce type de variations enrichit les possibilités typographiques—ce qui est fondamental dans les documents contemporains & la presse, où les commentaires & analyses doivent se démarquer subtilement de l'information elle-même. Le dessin du Le Monde Sans reprend la structure de base commune aux membres de la famille Le Monde: proportions, chasse relativement étroite, axe oblique moins appuyé, etc. Sans boulverser le texte, le typographe peut échanger les vers ons Sans & Journal. Ce style est décliné dans de nombreuses variantes de graisses—sept au total—en romain, italique & petites capitales pour faire face à toute sorte de situations. Malgré tout, standards sont conçues pour fonctionner parfaitement avec le reste des styles.

LE MONDE SANS THIN & ITALIC
àbcdéfghijklmñôpqrstùvwxyz
àbcdéfghijklmñôpqrstùvwxyz
ABCDEFGHIJKLMNOPQRSTUVWXYZ
0123456789 & 0123456789 ßfiflßfjfl«‹!?.,;:'»

LE MONDE SANS LIGHT & ITALIC
àbcdéfghijklmñôpqrstùvwxyz
àbcdéfghijklmñôpqrstùvwxyz
ABCDEFGHIJKLMNOPQRSTUVWXYZ
0123456789 & 0123456789 ßfiflßfjfl«‹!?.,;:'»

LE MONDE SANS NORMAL & ITALIC
àbcdéfghijklmñôpqrstùvwxyz
àbcdéfghijklmñôpqrstùvwxyz
ABCDEFGHIJKLMNOPQRSTUVWXYZ
ABCDEFGHIJKLMNOPQRSTUVWXYZ
0123456789 & 0123456789 ßfiflßfjfl«‹!?.,;:'»

LE MONDE SANS SEMI BOLD & ITALIC
àbcdéfghijklmñôpqrstùvwxyz
àbcdéfghijklmñôpqrstùvwxyz
ABCDEFGHIJKLMNOPQRSTUVWXYZ
ABCDEFGHIJKLMNOPQRSTUVWXYZ
0123456789 & 0123456789 ßfiflßfjfl«‹!?.,;:'»

LE MONDE SANS BOLD & ITALIC
àbcdéfghijklmñôpqrstùvwxyz
àbcdéfghijklmñôpqrstùvwxyz
ABCDEFGHIJKLMNOPQRSTUVWXYZ
ABCDEFGHIJKLMNOPQRSTUVWXYZ
0123456789 & 0123456789 ßfiflßfjfl«‹!?.,;:'»

Initial approach and development

A number of factors played a part in Porchez's development of Parisine, the main ideas of which, he says, came into his head very quickly. 'I already had the ten-per-cent condensed as a basis, and I knew that faces like Frutiger (created for the signage of the Roissy Charles de Gaulle Airport in Paris, during the 1970s) were very legible for signage, so that acted as a reference,' explains Porchez.

He had also just finished Le Monde Sans, a sanserif face which was to act as body copy (i.e. in very small sizes) for French national newspaper *Le Monde*, an experience which led him to believe that 'contrasts and open counters are crucial'. While Frutiger features these open counters, Porchez believes it lacks the contrast – perhaps because Adrian Frutiger is originally from Switzerland, a country in which three nationalities and their languages co-exist, leading him "to universalise" his forms. I don't have the same references, mine are more Latin,' says Porchez.

While looking for a solution to the problem of narrow proportions, Porchez says his model was the typeface created by Johnston for the London Underground in 1917. 'The people at RATP liked the idea of this for two reasons; Johnston has been used for all signage and communication material on London transport for almost 100 years now, and RATP use Gill Sans for their corporate communication system... I gave them a link by pointing out that Eric Gill was a pupil of Edward Johnston, and in doing so, I found a very valuable argument! I told them that I would create a typeface which mixed the quality of Helvetica condensed with the humanity of Gill Sans!'

3 On site, the difference between the old Helvetica signs and the new Parisine ones are more obvious: there is better contrast between the forms; the d and b are different in their counterforms, the Parisine g is more specific than the g of Helvetica and i dots are round to improve the overall picture formed by the word.

↓ (RER) (B) **Aéroport Ch. de Gaulle** [CDG]
Mitry – Clay • Robinson
Antony [Orly] **• St-Rémy-lès-Chevreuses**

↑

(M) (6) **Ch. de Gaulle – Étoile**
Nation

← **Sortie**

1 **bd Auguste Blanqui**
  Manufacture des Gobelins

2 **Grand Écran**

3 **bd Vincent Auriol**

4 **av. Augustin Dumont**

Helvetica

↓ (RER) (B) **Aéroport Ch. de Gaulle** [CDG]
Mitry – Clay • Robinson
Antony [Orly] **• St-Rémy-lès-Chevreuses**

↑

(M) (6) **Ch. de Gaulle – Étoile**
Nation

← **Sortie**

1 **bd Auguste Blanqui**
  Manufacture des Gobelins

2 **Grand Écran**

3 **bd Vincent Auriol**

4 **av. Augustin Dumont**

Parisine

(RER) (A) St-Germain-en-Laye • Poissy
Cergy • Boissy-St-Léger
Marne-la-Vallée

(B) Aéroport Ch. de Gaulle [CDG]
Mitry – Clay [Orly]
Robinson • Antony
St-Rémy-lès-Chevreuse

Montigny – Beauchamp – Argenteuil
Versailles – Rive Gauche
Versailles – Chantiers • St-Quentin
Massy - Palaiseau • Dourdan • St-Ma...

(C) Orry-la-Ville
(D) Melun
Malesherbes

(M) (11) Châtelet
Mairie des Lilas

(12) Pte de La Chapelle
Mairie d'Issy

(13) Asnières – Gennevilliers
Saint-Denis • Châtillon

(14) Madeleine
Bibliothèque

(T) (1) Saint-Denis
Bobigny

Le Parisine, une grande famille d
Le Parisine, une grande famille de

Le Parisine, une grande famille de
Le Parisine, une grande famille de c

Le Parisine, une grande famille de ca
Le Parisine, une grande famille de carac

Le Parisine, une grande famille de cara
Le Parisine, une grande famille de caract

Le Parisine, une grande famille de caracte
Le Parisine, une grande famille de caract

Le Parisine, une grande famille de caractè
Le Parisine, une grande famille de caracté

The font

'It is a fact that Helvetica is not the best or more legible typeface. Open typefaces like Frutiger are conceptually more legible because of the open forms of the terminals a, e and s,' says Porchez. 'With Parisine I proposed better legibility and also better contrast between the forms than Frutiger and Helvetica: d, b, p and q are different in their counterforms, g (like in Gill Sans) is more specific than g (like in Helvetica and Frutiger), i dots are round to improve word picture, the word shape is more contrasted (necessary because Parisine is narrower), the terminal of the a, the f and t are wider than would be on a strict narrow face, as are the capital letters and figures. The caps are also shorter than the ascenders to help word shape recognition. Studies on legibility prove that our eyes "read" the top third of the x-height, so with contrasted terminals (on obliques, not verticals or horizontals) and more emphasis on certain letters and accents, Parisine is more legible than Helvetica. The punctuation was also developed to work well in the large signage size... more fluent, softer, less constructed and technical.'

4 This year, Porchez completed the Parisine family with six new weights, for use in RATP maps and information material.

4

Parisine, new programme 1999

Clair Regular — *Parisine Parisine*

Clair Bold — *Parisine Parisine*

Regular — Parisine *Parisine*

Bold — **Parisine Parisine**

Sombre — **Parisine** *Parisine*

Sombre Bold — **Parisine Parisine**

PORCHEZ *Typofonderie*

'BECAUSE PARISINE WAS BASED ON HELVETICA, MY FIRST STEP WAS TO USE HELVETICA... BUT NOT IN THE "COPY AND PASTE" STYLE OF THOSE TRASHY SHAREWARE FONTS, WHOSE DESIGNERS DISREGARD THINGS LIKE COPYRIGHT.'

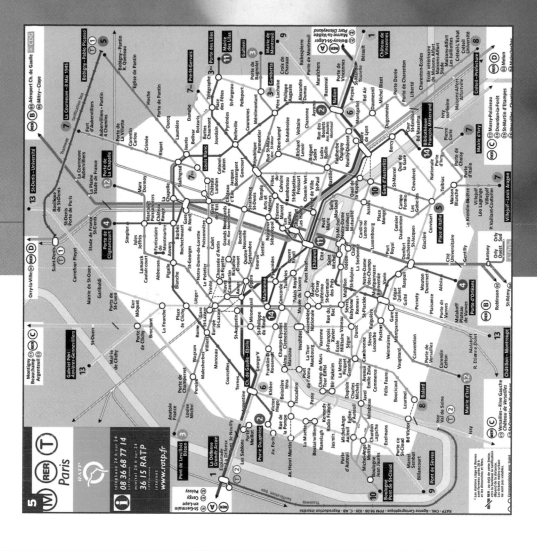

5 Although originally intended just for signage, Parisine is now being adopted throughout the RATP system after successful testing in maps and other literature.

6 The standardised typeface and colours on the station route map and on-train route planner allow fast recognition and make planning easier.

The Working Process

Rather than go through laborious roughs and a lengthy process of creative steps, Porchez designs the basis for most of his fonts directly on screen and very quickly; 'Adjustments such as spacing, kerning etc. take much longer, but the initial ideas and forms present themselves quickly', he says. 'Also, this face is based on a reworking of Helvetica, so the first step was Helvetica itself!'

But he stresses that the computer program is just that; 'the forms and shapes of the letters come from the head and hand of the designer, and it's the most important point. Bézier curves are only a tool for rendering the forms of the typefaces we create,' he says emphatically. Currently he's using Macromedia Fontographer and Robofog, past dalliances have included URW Ikarus, future ones Pyrus FontLab; 'the tools are important but if the current tool doesn't provide what I need, I don't have a problem switching. We can't systematically use only one software for all situations: Just say no to software drug dependency!' advises Porchez.

Because Parisine was initially to be used just for signage, once it was designed one of the first steps was to test it very quickly to see if the face worked on the enamel metal panels

(plaques emaillées). And legibility was easy to test; 'because Helvetica is already used in the new signage system, I had a very good example of what I needed to do to optimise the legibility!' says Porchez. Since the first two weights – bold and bold italic – in 1996, RATP has tested the font for small-size use on maps and information material, and last year asked Porchez to design a Regular and Regular Italic. He responded with a proposal to create an entire family of six weights, convinced that the two weights were not enough and would prove restrictive in the future. The difference in terms of budget is not that great, and it's better to design all the weights together than a new one each year.' Porchez's eventual hope is to see Parisine used also for advertising and external communication in the near future, and he believes that the new weights are already allowing better use in a growing number of applications, for example 'the extra-bold is now finished and has been tested for specific use on maps, and it provides a better contrast when used with the regular than bold and regular do when used together.' It's likely that come the millennium, visitors to Paris will enjoy a standardised transport signage system to rival that of London – and maybe visitors to London will enjoy a transport system to rival that of Paris!

'THE TOOLS ARE IMPORTANT BUT, IF THE CURRENT TOOL DOESN'T PROVIDE WHAT I NEED, I DON'T HAVE A PROBLEM SWITCHING. WE CAN'T SYSTEMATICALLY USE ONLY ONE SOFTWARE FOR ALL SITUATIONS: JUST SAY NO TO SOFTWARE DRUG DEPENDENCY!'

DETAILS
Jean-François Porchez
Porchez Typofonderie
38 bis avenue Augustin-Dumont
92240 Ma akcff, France
tel/fax: +33 146 542 692
email: info@pcrcheztpo.com
http://www.porcheztypo.com/

HARDWARE/SOFTWARE
Mac G3 266, Powerbook 1400 and two printers: Apple 600DPI A4 and HP 1200DPI A3.
Macromedia Fontographer, URW Ikarus and Robofog.
'And softwindows to emulate Windows on my Mac, which allows me to use some Windows software to finish some fonts!'

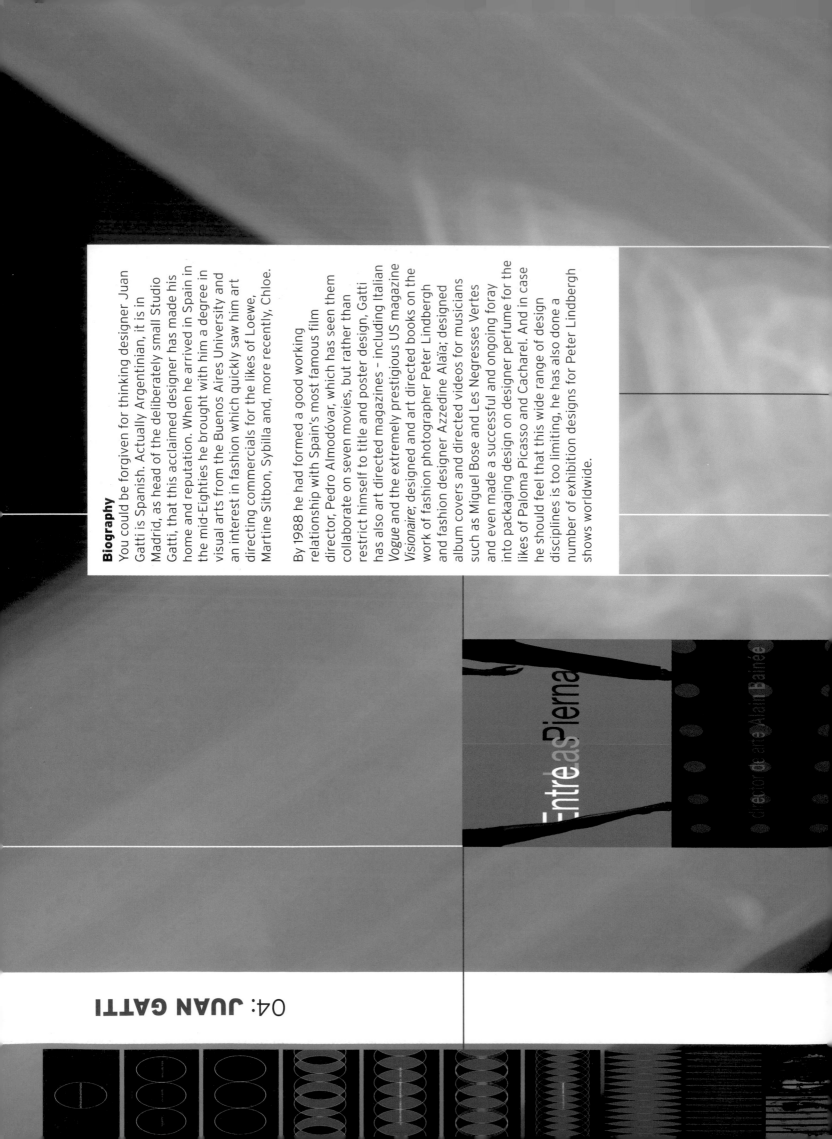

Biography

You could be forgiven for thinking designer Juan Gatti is Spanish. Actually Argentinian, it is in Madrid, as head of the deliberately small Studio Gatti, that this acclaimed designer has made his home and reputation. When he arrived in Spain in the mid-Eighties he brought with him a degree in visual arts from the Buenos Aires University and an interest in fashion which quickly saw him art directing commercials for the likes of Loewe, Martine Sitbon, Sybilla and, more recently, Chloe.

By 1988 he had formed a good working relationship with Spain's most famous film director, Pedro Almodóvar, which has seen them collaborate on seven movies, but rather than restrict himself to title and poster design, Gatti has also art directed magazines – including Italian *Vogue* and the extremely prestigious US magazine *Visionaire*; designed and art directed books on the work of fashion photographer Peter Lindbergh and fashion designer Azzedine Alaïa; designed album covers and directed videos for musicians such as Miguel Bose and Les Negresses Vertes and even made a successful and ongoing foray into packaging design on designer perfume for the likes of Paloma Picasso and Cacharel. And in case he should feel that this wide range of design disciplines is too limiting, he has also done a number of exhibition designs for Peter Lindbergh shows worldwide.

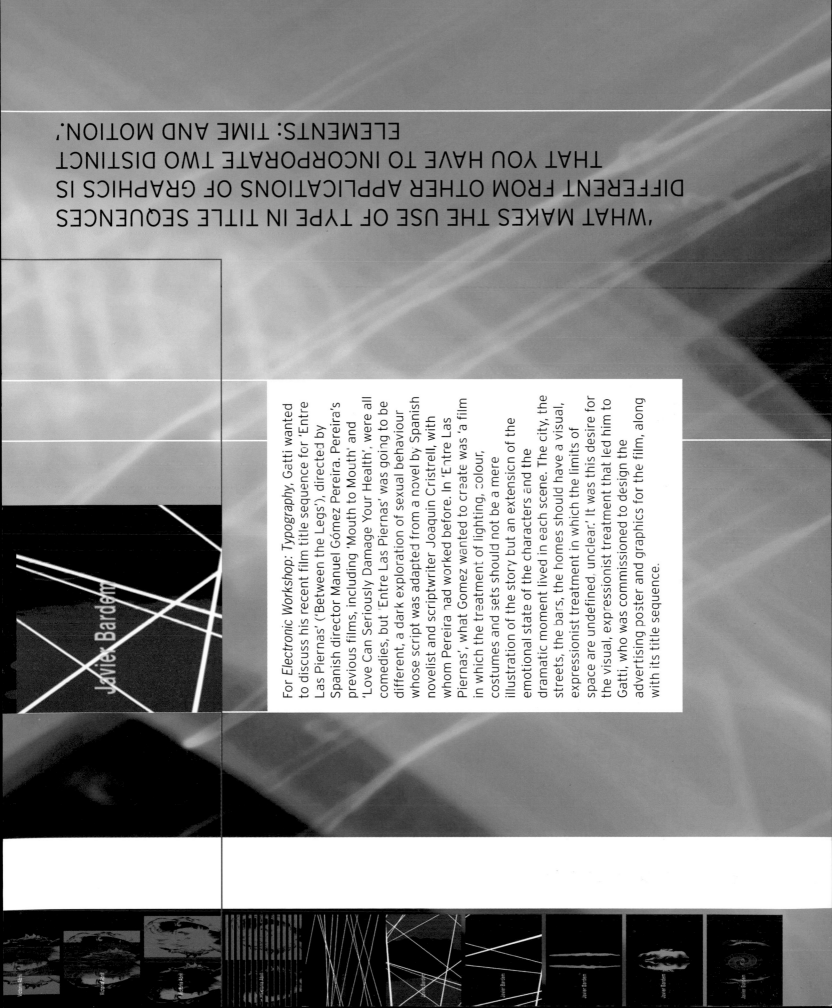

For *Electronic Workshop: Typography*, Gatti wanted to discuss his recent film title sequence for 'Entre Las Piernas' ('Between the Legs'), directed by Spanish director Manuel Gómez Pereira. Pereira's previous films, including 'Mouth to Mouth' and 'Love Can Seriously Damage Your Health', were all comedies, but 'Entre Las Piernas' was going to be different, a dark exploration of sexual behaviour whose script was adapted from a novel by Spanish novelist and scriptwriter Joaquin Cristrell, with whom Pereira had worked before. In 'Entre Las Piernas', what Gomez wanted to create was 'a film in which the treatment of lighting, colour, costumes and sets should not be a mere illustration of the story but an extension of the emotional state of the characters and the dramatic moment lived in each scene. The city, the streets, the bars, the homes should have a visual, expressionist treatment in which the limits of space are undefined, unclear.' It was this desire for the visual, expressionist treatment that led him to Gatti, who was commissioned to design the advertising poster and graphics for the film, along with its title sequence.

Javier Bardem

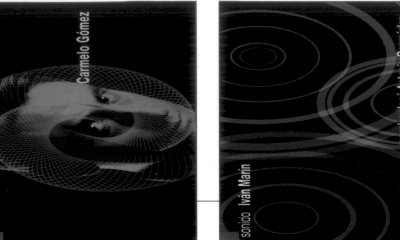

1

Carmelo Gómez

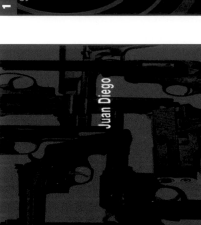

1

sonido Iván Marín

mezclas José Antonio Bermúdez

1

pub BOCABOCA PRODUCCIONES S.A. - AURUM PRODUCCIONES S.A. - D.M.V.B. FILMS

1

Juan Diego

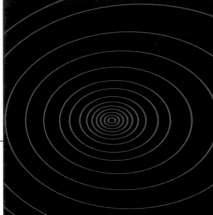

2

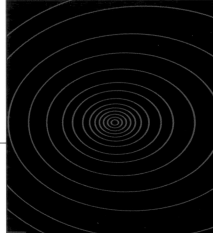

2

1 In 'Entre Las Piernas', Gatti decided to make the typography 'very classic and minimalist, so as to simply give information rather than compete with the background images,' he explains. 'In other works, I have given type a leading role and it has packed all the emotional punch,' he adds.

Initial approach and development

'The story of "Entre Las Piernas" can best be described as a pyschological thriller,' says Gatti of the story, which centres on the characters and relationships of Javier and Miranda, two people who meet at a group therapy session for sex addicts. Their relationship is destined to involve murder, obsession and sexual fantasies, and it was this that attracted Gatti: 'What interested me in the case of "Entre Las Piernas" was to convey an obsessive, hypnotic atmosphere in which not only figurative, but also abstract and geometric elements would convey a climate of suspicion and make great play of the idea of layers and overlays as hidden things. I got the first ideas for the work from reading the script and then from seeing some rushes of what had been filmed.'

Gatti always begins with the script and consultation with the director, who in this case 'was personally involved in the design, but gave me complete freedom,' he says. Generally, Gatti's ideas, he explains, 'will come from the store of images I have built up over a lifetime spent devouring images of every kind – cinema, fashion magazines, posters in the street, animation, TV, etc. etc.' He admits that fashion and trends 'do influence designs, of course, and sometimes fashions and trends arise in title sequences, which is something to be avoided,' he advises.

2 The story of the movie focuses a lot on technology and surveillance, for example taped conversations of Javier's erotic phone relationship with an unknown woman are being circulated widely through Madrid. The sound waves and iconography of the titles reflect this.

3 Interlinking circles are stretched and narrowed to metamorphisise into vertical venetian blinds through which we first see Victoria Abril, who plays the sex addict Miranda, one of the film's main protagonists.

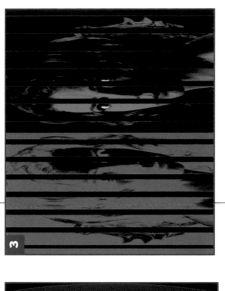

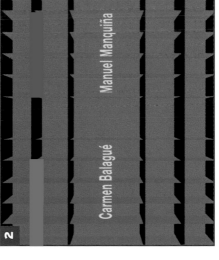

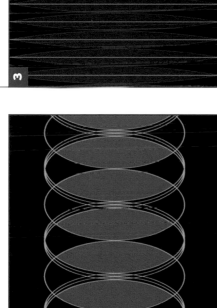

'WITH "ENTRE LAS PIERNAS" I WANTED TO CONVEY AN OBSESSIVE, HYPNOTIC ATMOSPHERE IN WHICH NOT ONLY FIGURATIVE, BUT ALSO ABSTRACT AND GEOMETRIC ELEMENTS, WOULD CONVEY A CLIMATE OF SUSPICION AND MAKE GREAT PLAY OF THE IDEA OF LAYERS AND OVERLAYS AS HIDDEN THINGS.'

montaje José Salcedo

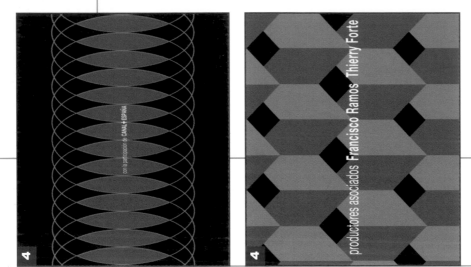

con la participación de CANAL+ESPAÑA

productores asociados Francisco Ramos Thierry Forte

maquillaje Ana Lozano

sonido Iván Marín

mezclas José Antonio Bermúdez

Working process and techniques

While shooting on the movie was still in progress, Gatti was given a script, but did not actually start working on the storyboard and images until shooting of the movie was completed. 'At that point, I began my work; commencing with a photo session with the leading actors. I took the pictures myself to use for the poster as well as the press book and advertising,' he explains.

After the photo session Gatti began the storyboard, 'using good old pencil and paper,' he laughs. 'After that was finished most of the toning and processing of the photographic material used was done in Photoshop, while I did some geometric compositions and text in Freehand. Animation was done in Inferno. In addition, for some of the effects I wanted, we had to set up a program which had 3D elements and was animated using Inferno,' recalls Gatti.

4 Perspective, waves and geometric patterns run throughout the title sequence, bringing to mind the classic psychological thrillers of the cold war era of America in the 1950s and '60s, when directors like John Frankenheimer and Alfred Hitchcock were capturing the unspoken sense of paranoia that pervaded the US.

5 The frames containing the production credits wittily visually reinforce the particular role being credited, while remaining in keeping with the narrative structure of the sequence.

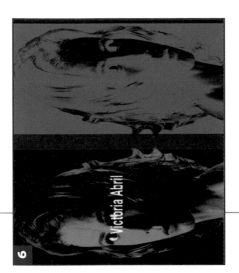

Victoria Abril

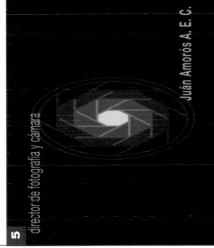

5 | director de fotografía y cámara

Juán Amorós A. E. C.

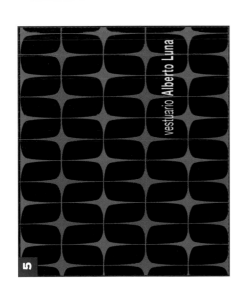

5 | vestuario **Alberto Luna**

6 | Javier Bardem

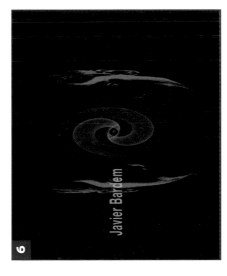

6 | Javier Bardem

6 | Manuel Gómez Pereira, director of 'Entre las Piernas', said of the film: 'The style can be none other than that undoubtedly used in the novel, which unites all the elements of mystery literature, starting with the most powerful of an undefined genre known as the novel of *cinema noir*.' Gatti's titles echo those perennial themes of noir such as duplicity and intrigue.

'I THINK THAT, APART FROM INFORMING THE AUDIENCE, THE TITLE SEQUENCE SHOULD SET THE SCENE, PUT THEM IN THE MOOD AND CAPTIVATE THEM. WHAT REALLY MAKES A GREAT TITLE SEQUENCE IS THE TALENT OF THE PERSON WHO MAKES IT.'

director de producción **Alejandro Vázquez**

7 Gatti has managed to incorporate the dense colour and multi-layered textures which are the defining factor of much of his work for Pedro Almodóvar's title sequences.

'In this film, the use of typography was very classic and minimalist, so as to simply give information rather than compete with the background images. In other works, I have given type a leading role and it has packed all the emotional punch.'

Sergi López

'I NEVER GO NEAR A COMPUTER WITHOUT A CLEAR OUTLINE OF MY IDEAS. IT IS TRUE THAT NEW TECHNOLOGY IS NECESSARY IN PRACTICAL TERMS, BUT ONLY PROVIDED YOU USE IT TO GIVE YOUR IMAGINATION FREE REIN.'

'As regards my work with technology, I try to use it for my ideas and it is part of a stage after the creative process – I never go near a computer without a clear outline of my ideas. It is true that new technology is necessary in practical terms, but only provided you use it to give your imagination free rein,' he insists.

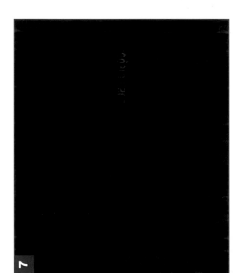

8 The background image for the 'Entre Las Piernas' poster and the finished poster.

9 Gatti experimented with a number of ideas for the poster's script.

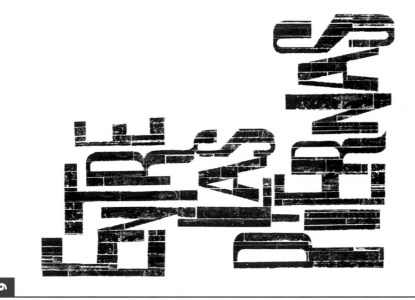

9

8

9

ENTRE LAS PIERNAS

8

VICTORIA ABRIL JAVIER BARDEM CARMELO GOMEZ

ENTRE LAS PIERNAS

DIRIGIDA POR MANUEL GOMEZ PEREIRA

9

ENTRE LAS PIERNAS

DETAILS
Stud o Gatti
C/Puigcerdá Nº 14
28001 - Madrid
Spain
tel/fax: +34 915 75 18 02
e-mail: gatti@ctv.es

HARDWARE/SOFTWARE
Photoshop, Freehand, Inferno, Flame.

'OUR FIRST IMPRESSIONS AND INITIAL DECISIONS ABOUT THE GRAPHICS ARE BASED ON THE CONTENT, THEN WE'LL GO THROUGH FONT BOOKS, OR START PLAYING AROUND WITH METAL TYPE, EVEN LETRASET, WHATEVER WE THINK MIGHT SUIT THE FEEL OF THE CONTENT AND THE PHYSICAL SPACE IN WHICH IT'S LOCATED.'

Biography

Exhibition design has become huge business in the last couple of decades, with branding and banner design playing an important role in fuelling the excitement and imagination of audiences who will queue overnight to see expensive animatronics and play with intricate interactives. And one London consultancy is responsible for a large amount of these 'total experience' exhibitions; MET Studio Design can justifiably lay claim to some of the most imaginative and radical exhibition design in the world, with clients spanning the globe from London's Science Museum and Natural History Museum to Hong Kong's Urban Services Department and the National Museum of Science and Technology in Taiwan. Many of its exhibitions have won awards in areas as diverse as lighting, environment, multimedia programmes and educational initiatives – and of course exhibition design.

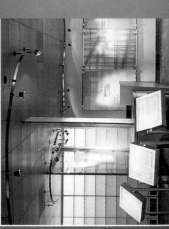

Background

But until this year MET had never unveiled an exhibition project in North America. In March, however, The Field Museum in Chicago turned its basement into The Underground Experience, a $10m attraction incorporating several diverse spaces over 15,000 square feet. Unusually, as it had never before appointed an outside design group for such a large-scale project. The museum held a four-way pitch which was won by the only non-US design group, MET Studio Design, who created the exhibition in partnership with the museum's own in-house design and development team. The 106-year-old Field Museum is dedicated to building understanding of the diversity and interconnections in nature, across cultures and between people and their environment. With the Underground Experience it wanted to get across the importance of soil in the life of the earth and its inhabitants in an informative yet entertaining way – something of a tall order when most people probably think of soil as unpleasant stuff full of unpleasant creatures. Getting beyond those kinds of feelings to create an entertaining, educational and experience-based space which people would actually want to visit was MET's task, and from her first site visit, senior designer Helen Lyon knew that it was a huge one: 'Initial impressions weren't great, the space was a huge basement with no natural light, and I just looked around and thought "how can this possibly be turned into anything that's going to be really exciting and interesting?"'

Initial approach, development and working process

As the museum had already decided on the storyline, content and space, MET's first task was to outline and work up a script for the 'experience', which was basically the visitor being shrunk and journeying through the soil to be confronted with huge bugs, grubs and pollen spores before emerging into a 'research facility'. 'The brief was quite constrained, but in developing the script we had a lot of scope. All it needed was "Americanisation", or made more appropriate to a US audience. We were able to draw on the experience of the Museum staff to help us with this,' says Lyon.

Lyon's and MET's director of graphics, Pat O'Leary, along with MET architects and 3D designers, had a series of meetings with the client to discuss the exhibition's content, before drawing up mood-boards for the four major concept areas of the Underground Experience: Base Camp, the Microscopic Laboratory, The Mud Room and Soil Connections. Other smaller spaces such as the exhibition entrance, the Transmogrifier Rooms and the closing Conclusions area were also to be created by MET. 'My initial fears were allayed as we began to bounce ideas around; the architects and 3D people were very helpful there, in helping us understand the space better. They at this stage had been working on the project for some two to three months, so already had a really good overview of it,' explains Lyon. The mood-boards aimed to give a very general feel for the space, with possible key colours, textures and materials which might successfully relate to and translate the space. 'Along with the boards, were specific thoughts and ideas, though again quite general observations. For example, in a content-heavy space we suggested the museum might want more playful illustrations and graphics to gently help the visitor cope with the barrage of information they were receiving,' says Lyon.

After this phase the graphics team worked up scheme designs, essentially broad themes for the graphic treatments on the separate areas which, after client assessment and approval, were made more detailed: 'Colours, dummy text, illustrations and any other graphic devices would be added before putting the whole graphics package out to tender. The chosen company would then receive a final artwork package from us,' says Lyon.

Through all of the early development stages Lyon is constantly trying to balance the integrity of the design with graphic legibility and accessibility: 'Legibility is extremely important – if you want the visitor to read the text you must make it easy for them. Lighting, font size, leading – for large script text has to have a lot of leading in it, colours have to be carefully put together. For example, you don't put red and green together because for colour-blind visitors these two colours are the hardest to differentiate. Things like choice of typefaces have to be well thought out too. This exhibition will be here for 20 years, and if I'd chosen a really fashionable typeface it would look very dated very quickly. In terms of size, I would have liked to use smaller type, but had to enlarge both size and leading to comply with the museum's guidelines.'

MET's concept was to create a street feel for the underground space, and a lot of that would be done through the graphics and typefaces used: 'Rather than a more obvious grotto-like space dotted with big lumps of soil, we wanted a sense of energy about the space, to look at underground as being about mining, transportation and alternative urban environments. There had to be an element of fun, with bright colours, chevrons and warning notices making the space more exciting, and hopefully creating the opposite of people's preconceptions about soil and underground activity,' says Lyon. 'We were aware that in some cases and spaces we had to separate the graphics from the environment, while in others the two had to be integrated; for example, in the underground [Micro-Soil Lab] space, the graphics had to contrast strongly with the soil, animatronics and general space, while in the research area [Mud Room] with its parquet floors and racking system, the graphics had to merge with the environment in a complementary way to suggest a scientific, futuristic research centre,' she explains.

Entrance area and Base Camp

MET studio's first task with the exhibition was to attract people into it, and as the museum has its own corporate signage system it opted to eschew conflicting and potentially confusing signs in favour of banners which would clearly signpost the way to the Underground Experience and start to familiarise visitors with the environment. 'Obviously we wanted to grab people's interest here, so display cases hold objects you wouldn't normally associate with soil and explain its relationship with them, everyday things like aluminium cans, jeans, cereals and medicine,' says Lyon. Beyond this area visitors encounter a graphics panel which is intended to take them from city to a soil research station sited on the prairie on which Chicago is built – as they descend, the scenes change from pipes and concrete skyscrapers to crops and soil. 'It's a minimalist, airy space whose minimalism wasn't entirely intentional,' says Lyon, adding 'we planned to have more in it, but time and budget constraints meant that we did lose a few of the original concepts. That's not necessarily a bad thing as it makes you think hard about the value of every single aspect and piece of any given project.' It was in the Base Camp that MET encountered its first problems with the client: 'We'd developed the idea of a multi-layered space with lots of textures, but the client found some of this too overpowering, so we had to go with a very clean, bright and pure space. However, it does at least retain an essence of the rawness we were aiming for in the locker wall,' says Lyon.

1 The graphics panel leading the visitor from the entrance to the Base Camp area is an early example of MET's first concept of the journey from Chicago to the camp. 'The initial ideas are always the wildest, but these change and evolve along with the storyline and the 3D Design,' says Lyon (far left).

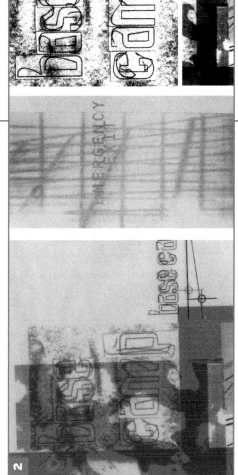

2 Lyon's grungy, muddy typeface for the Base Camp was cleaned up considerably before client approval. The space acts as a research centre where cutting-edge work is being undertaken by scientists keen to learn more about living soil systems and their conservation.

3 'We'd developed the idea of a multi-layered space with lots of textures for this area, but it was rejected so we had to go with a very clean, bright and pure space. It does at least retain an essence of the rawness we were aiming for in the locker wall,' says Lyon.

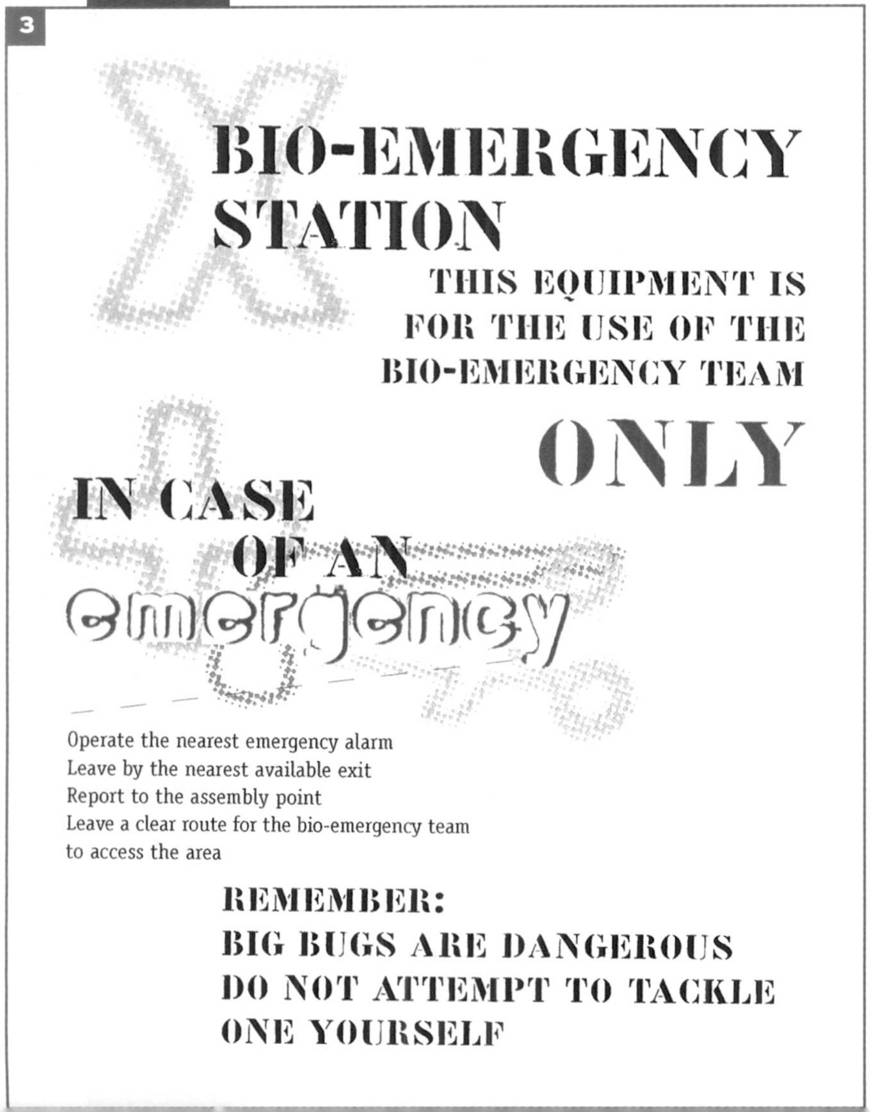

1

FIRST AID

2

UNDERGROUND RESCUE

BIO-EMERGENCY STATION

THIS EQUIPMENT IS FOR THE USE OF THE BIO-EMERGENCY TEAM ONLY

IN CASE OF AN emergency

Operate the nearest emergency alarm

Leave by the nearest available exit

Report to the assembly point

Leave a clear route for the bio-emergency team to access the area

REMEMBER:

BIG BUGS ARE DANGEROUS

DO NOT ATTEMPT TO TACKLE ONE YOURSELF

'THE GRAPHIC APPROACH IN THIS GALLERY IS RADICALLY DIFFERENT FROM ALL THE OTHER GALLERIES IN THE FIELD MUSEUM. I THINK IT'S VERY MUCH TO OUR CLIENT'S CREDIT THAT, IN SPITE OF SOME COMPROMISE, THEY WERE BRAVE ENOUGH TO STAND BY OUR ORIGINAL CONCEPTS AND ALLOW US TO PRODUCE SUCH AN EXCITING EXHIBITION.'

PAT O'LEARY, MET'S DIRECTOR OF GRAPHICS

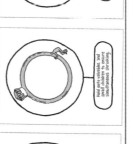

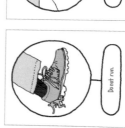

HELPFUL HINTS FOR SAFE SHRINKING

4 In the Ames Room, or transmogrifier, MET used a chequered floor to aid the illusion of shrinking, 'rather like an Escher drawing,' says Lyon. 'T'e mirrored corridor, flashing lights and lots of weird sounds are all geared to the sense of fun and adventure as you're supposed to be shrinking while you go through the transmogrifier,' she adds. The drawing shows the original idea for the panel seen in the finished space.

Micro-Soil Lab

The Micro-Soil Laboratory is the centrepiece of the Underground Experience. Here smell, sounds, animatronics and subdued lighting combine to give a sense of things moving and shifting, creating a temporary environment which was reflected in the graphics. Dotted throughout the space and along the walkway are information posts and study areas: 'These offered a great opportunity for some interesting graphics solutions. For example, using markings across the huts, suggesting animals having brushed against them. We also needed to come up with a labelling system in keeping with the research being carried out by our fictional scientists, and I used Dymo tape to reflect the sense of movement and temporary space,' says Lyon.

5 The Micro-Soil Lab uses a wide variety of materials and presented many graphics opportunities for the MET team, most of which made it through to the finished space, although as these drawings show, not without some alterations.

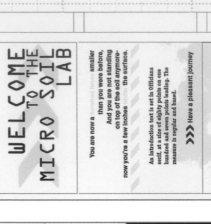

5

WELCOME TO THE MICRO SOIL LAB

You are now a hundred times smaller than you were before, And you are not standing on top of the soil anymore—now you're a few inches inside the surface.

An introduction text is set in Officiana serif, at a size of eighty points on one hundred and seven points leading. The measure is regular and based.

>>> Have a pleasant journey

shrink check station

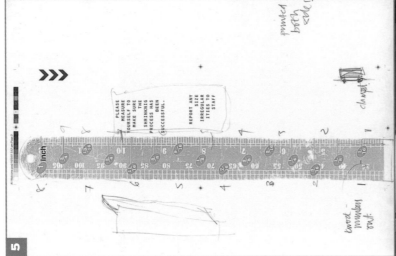

5

6 The Micro-Soil Lab environment is dotted with 'huts', which in the narrative of the Underground Experience are small underground research labs. Visitors are allowed a glimpse into the researchers' findings, studies etc.

7 The sense of flux and shift in the Micro-Soil Laboratory was echoed on the huts, which are covered with animal marks and tracks and labels bearing typography based on the Dymo labelling system. Muddy type aids the street feel of the space.

8 Information posts bearing strong graphics echo the street, utilitarian feel of the Micro-Soil Lab, and give directions and information on the insects the visitor is enjoying a reverse-microscopic view of, but also impart information about the soil's fabric, organisms and relationship with above-ground inhabitants.

6

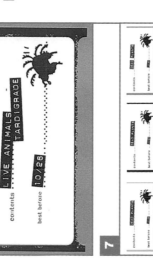
7

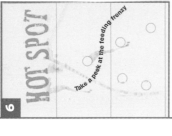
7

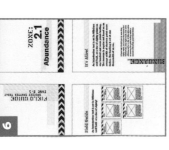
6

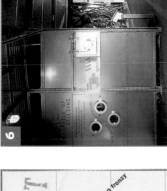
6

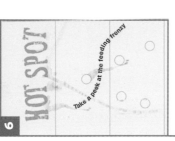
7

8

'THERE ARE RULES YOU HAVE TO ADHERE TO. WE ALWAYS MOCK-UP FULL-SIZE BLOCKS OF TEXT. WHEN THE CLIENT IS WRITING A SCRIPT WE GIVE THEM LINE LENGTHS, WORD COUNTS AND SO ON, BECAUSE IF YOU DESIGN A GRAPHIC PANEL TO A CERTAIN SIZE AND YOUR POINT SIZE IS SET THEN OBVIOUSLY YOU CAN ONLY FIT A SET AMOUNT OF WORDS ON IT. COPYWRITING TO THIS TYPE OF GUIDELINE IS NORMAL PRACTISE IN NEWSPAPER AND MAGAZINE DESIGN BUT NOT ALWAYS AN OBVIOUS APPROACH TO EXHIBITION DESIGN.'

9 'For the Mud Room I did this muddy typeface, based on some plastic letters I'd bought which were then cut up and made into a stamp, like a Billy stamp, which was really nice to do,' explains Lyon.

10 'In the Mud Room, we had an exhibit called "Label Yourself" which was about labelling collections in the museum, and I wanted to get a real typewriter feel to it. We got a lot of reference material from the museum about how they label things, and this was part of the inspiration behind our graphic approach for this area.'

The Mud Room

The large interactive area visitors emerge into after being re-transmogrified to full size in some ways offered the MET graphics team the best environment of all the spaces: 'Here the connections between everything you learned underground and yourself are explained, so it's heavily exhibit-based, has lots of interactives and is very tactile. Because its purpose is to enable understanding, we were able to design lots of nice informative graphic panels, whose only downside is the difficulty in working them up convincingly on-screen; it gets easier with practice but you still have to print out an awful lot of proofs,' laughs Lyon.

Designed like a lab storage area, the Mud Room's walls are covered in racking systems which bear containers filled with interactives and information. The pure sci-fi feel of the space contrasted with the contents of the containers to give MET plenty of room for diversity in the space: 'We went from very clean to muddy grungy display types and back again, because the sheer volume of information in there allowed and encouraged it,' says Lyon. 'I think the importance of total integration between graphics and the 3D design is not stressed enough. It's too easy to stick up a panel with black text on a white background with some little illustration. This still happens far too much. It's getting better, with designers and museums becoming far more adventurous, but the type can help tell the story, as can the colours, and both can reflect the content and the space. In this particular exhibition, the content is actually quite heavy going, and can be difficult for the visitor to get his head around, I think it needed softening, and we generally styled the main titles to give you a feel for the subject matter. Overall, I think we did a fantastic job!' she concludes.

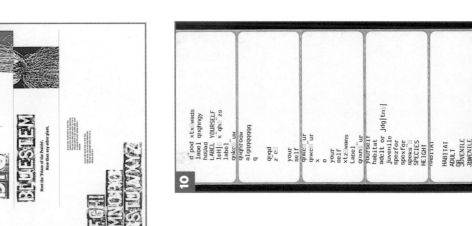

11 The sheer wealth of graphics and a myriad range of textures and surfaces offered MET a great opportunity for an inventive range of work.

SOFTWARE
Adobe Freehand, Photoshop, Apple kit.

DETAILS
MET Studio
6-8 Stardard Place
Rivington Street
London
EC2A 3BE
UK
tel: +44 171 7294949
fax: +44 171 7291638

Biography

Dutch typographer Luc(as) de Groot, creator of fonts including Thesis, TheSans and Jesus Loves You All, recently set up his own design bureau, FontFabrik. Luc(as) had worked for the well-known Meta agency in Berlin for many years, but in 1997 he received three simultaneous commissions and decided it was time to go it alone. De Groot's clients, for which he has developed custom fonts, have included Der Spiegel, Sun Microsystems and Bell South. His other fonts include MoveMe MultipleMaster, Typewriter, TheAntiquaB and the radical BolletjeWol.

'IT'S MY THEORY THAT NUMBERS COME FROM THE ARABIC WHILE LETTERS COME FROM ROMAN SCRIPT, SO THEY USED TO BE A DIFFERENT LANGUAGE AND SOMETIMES IT'S VERY GOOD TO KEEP THIS DISTINCT LANGUAGE'

In 1996, the Dutch ministry of Agriculture, Nature Management and Fishing – or Ministrie van Landbouw, Natuurbeheer en Visserij – commissioned Dutch design bureau Studio Dumbar to update its corporate identity. Studio Dumbar had not only worked on the ministry's existing corporate identity some ten years previously, but had also created new corporate identities for the Dutch royal mail and telecoms (at the time a single entity) and the Dutch national railway. The ministry, simultaneously expanding into new departments (meaning lots of new computers) and automating all its processes, was looking at the rather expensive proposition of licensing the Frutiger typeface for all its PCs, and found it prohibitively expensive.

Studio Dumbar asked De Groot to come on board because 'the ministry needed a fresh start,' says Maarten Jurriaanse, a designer at Studio Dumbar. Also, says Maarten, 'Luc(as) had done some similar work for the German subway, and he knows very well how to use a typeface.' De Groot and Studio Dumbar felt it would be easier – and cheaper – to create a totally new typeface based on Frutiger. 'It's always the thing: when you do something new, you have to invent everything,' says Maarten, 'but we convinced the ministry of the value of this,' their own unique typeface, 'so when you see the font, it's not just Helvetica, there's something different… subliminal.' 'Part of the assignment was to make something not too far away from Frutiger,' says De Groot, 'about the same colour of text and the same widths and sizes, globally. The amount of money wasn't very big – less than they would have spent licensing Frutiger – but I liked the assignment: it was interesting.'

The project

Maarten and De Groot first attacked the ministry's logo, beginning in late 1998. At the time, says Maarten, 'The ministry was using films or prints. It had no digitalised logos. We had to restructure the whole thing into a new, more modern structure.' Thus their next, far more difficult task entailed creating a four-part manual on how to implement the new identity. 'The next part was to make six fonts,' says De Groot, 'three weights plus italics – of course, the first part of the job was to make it print, with PostScript fonts, so the design bureau could start making the design, and could start printing some stuff. And the final part was to optimise the fonts for screen, which turned out to be the biggest part. It took me about two years.'

'I think I started with some outlines,' says De Groot. 'Bold italic was the last font I hinted. I started it only six months ago, but by that time I had learned so many tricks that I started all over again with this weight. I threw all the existing hints away and I even made partially new outlines to make better hints. Now the font is finished, the quality is really very, very good.'

1 'Frutiger Roman' (top), 'Agro Normaal' (bottom): this was the first presentation of the new design.

2 The corporate design of the ministry was designed by Studio Dumbar some 20 years ago, with Frutiger as the 'house font'. As in many corporations, with the introduction of desktop computers this automatically changed into Arial for all literature that was produced in-house, thereby diluting the corporate identity. Part of the brief was to aproach the colour and setting of the old fonts to facilitate the conversion for the publications that were permanently being produced by various desktop publishing units, and to introduce a company-wide uniform typographic quality. The idea was to make them work well in a digital world.

3 'Frutiger Bold' (first line); 'Agrofont-Vet' (second line); a refined version of Agrofont-Normaal (third line).

1

ABhamburgefnstickdalp

ABhamburgefnstickdalp

2

3

hamburgefonstickdjalpqv

hamburgefonstickdjalpqv

hamburgefonstickdjalpqv

4 'The first job was to finish all the logos,' says De Groot. 'It started off with a special version of the font, because it's a special weight and wider than the normal font.' Besides the ministry's own logo, each ministerial department also had a logo.

5 First presentation of the light weight. 'Light is always the most difficult family member. subtle weight changes in strokes come out clearest in light.'

6 First proposal for the italic. The glyphs a, e, f and the german double s have a different construction, characters bdqpq and hmnu also have italic flowing upstrokes.

7 'There's one more thing that helps in the screen display,' says De Groot, 'and that's the numbers, which jump a little bit, up and down. They're not classical, old-style figures, because classical, old-style figures have the looks of lower-case characters. But these are somewhere between classical old-style and table numbers, the size is somewhere in the middle between lower case and capitals.'

4

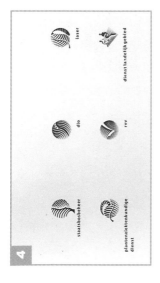

laser

dlo

rvv

dienst landelijk gebied

staatsbosbeheer

plantenziektenkundige dienst

4

5

abcdefg
hijklmno
pqrstuvw
xyzABCD
EFGHIJK
LVWXYZ
0123456
789

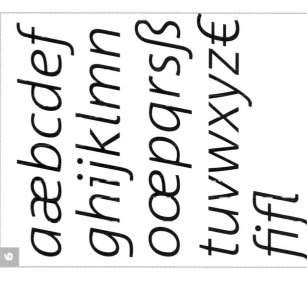

6

aæbcdef
ghijklmn
oœpqrsß
tuvwxyz£
fifl

7

rstuvwxyz1234567
890 !?.....:;,,"""

8 'The ministry is licensed to use Agrofont for two years and on January 1st, 2000, it becomes available in more weights. The version as it is now will be available 1st January but I plan to make at least a black weight.' At the moment it has light, normal and bold, and italics of each of these.

9 'We started out doing a logo for them, a square logo with an outline of Holland,' says Maarten.

10 'If you just make a standard conversion from a PostScript font to a TrueType font it looks horrible; you get very bad display quality.' This is what Agrofont looked like after 'autohinting' – what De Groot describes as 'dirty' and 'unusable in an office'.

'The ministry was using Agrofont on different kinds of machines,' says De Groot, 'and then all sorts of problems came up, like, "on this sort of printer we get this problem", or "in this program the line spacing is bigger than in that program". There's a lot of TrueType things that can go wrong the first time.' He went in to the ministry several times, and he says: 'At a certain point, when I thought the fonts work, they look very good on-screen, the ministry was still complaining about very detailed things – like, this character needs to move one pixel to the left'. At this point Studio Dumbar did something De Groot thought was 'a very good move; they hired an external company, Visualogic, to test and make a report about the font.' Visualogic itself makes technical fonts, and does hinting. 'This company thought the quality of the fonts was already very good,' says De Groot. 'But the project is not finished. The next step is to make some more weights. The typeface will be available in the year 2000,' he adds.

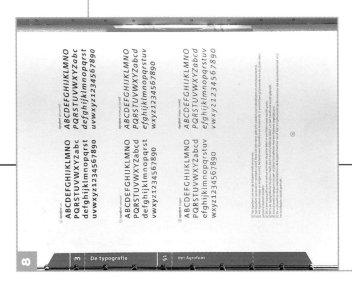

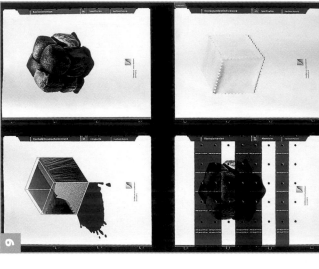

Development

'When I thought it was pretty good I sent it off to the ministry,' says De Groot. 'The difference was that I have a pretty big monitor and the ministry uses fairly cheap, small monitors, and when I was satisfied on my monitor they were not satisfied – that's why it took such a long time. They had it tested by ergonomics people and they said, "Arial is still better". It's a built-in PC font which is always taken as a comparison, and the reason is that a few guys at Monotype spent months hinting Arial, so it's perfect in all sizes. If you want to make a font that's as good as Arial, it really takes a long time.'

'Implementation is a very important part of corporate design,' says De Groot, 'and Dutch design bureaux are very, very good at this; they have a lot of experience at implementing this stuff on the workfloor. It's a political thing: you have to be a politician; you have to talk to the managers, tell them it's very important everyone uses the same fonts, and you have to show them that it's not too difficult to install all the fonts and that they work fine and they look good on-screen.'

10 8 ABCDEFGHIJKLMNOPQRSTUVWXZY 1234567890 abcdefghijklmnopqrsßuvwxzy @!?"§@®ƒ$¤%&/([{|}]) =ÄàÇçÉéÏïÖöÜü+*#.,:;-- The
9 ABCDEFGHIJKLMNOPQRSTUVWXZY 1234567890 abcdefghijklmnopqrsßuvwxzy @!?"§@®ƒ$¤%&/([{|}])=ÄàÇçÉéÏïÖöÜü+*#.,:;--
10 ABCDEFGHIJKLMNOPQRSTUVWXZY 1234567890 abcdefghijklmnopqrsßuvwxzy @!?"§@®ƒ$¤%&/([{|}]) =ÄàÇçÉéÏïÖöÜü+*#.,:;-- The quick brown fox jumps over the lazy dog lekker modderig 1999 is een fijn jaar
10½ ABCDEFGHIJKLMNOPQRSTUVWXZY 1234567890 abcdefghijklmnopqrsßuvwxzy @!?"§@®ƒ$¤%&/([{|}]) =ÄàÇçÉéÏïÖöÜü+*#.,:;-- The quick brown fox jumps over the lazy dog het is altweer een uur of 2:41:06 AM
11 ABCDEFGHIJKLMNOPQRSTUVWXZY 1234567890 abcdefghijklmnopqrsßuvwxzy @!?"§@®ƒ$¤%&/ ([{|}])=ÄàÇçÉéÏïÖöÜü+*#.,:;-- The quick brown fox jumps over the lazy dog Deze is wel heel erg vies
12 ABCDEFGHIJKLMNOPQRSTUVWXZY 1234567890 abcdefghijklmnopqrsßuvwxzy @!?"§@®ƒ$¤%&/([{|}]) =ÄàÇçÉéÏïÖöÜü+*#.,:;-- The quick brown fox jumps over the lazy dog Dat!zullewijlezenmoeten!
13 ABCDEFGHIQRSTUVWXZY 1234567890 abcdefghijklmnopqrsßuvwxzy @!?"§@®ƒ$¤%& /([{|}])=ÄàÇçÉéÏïÖöÜü The quick brown fox jumps over the lazy dog 90 cijfers plakken
14 ABCDEFGHIQRSTUVWXZY 1234567890 abcdefghijklmnopqrsßuvwxzy?"§@®ƒ $¤%&/([{|}])=ÄàÇçÉéÏï The quick brown fox jumps over the lazy dog oef zo'n prut
15 ABCDEFGHIQRSTUVWXZY 1234567890 abcdefghijklmnopqrsßuvwxzy @!?"§@®ƒ$¤%&/([{|}])= The quick brown fo jumps over the lazy dog

11 'The font after a lot of hinting hours... Each character is a little puzzle; you have to find little tricks to "solve" it in the most convenient way. There's a fast way if you have good "global" tricks, and you won't have to do a lot of delta hints – little "bumps". When you have done all your global tricks, if there's still a pixel too much you give a little bump in one corner to get rid of it. The better you do your global tricks, the fewer delta tricks you need.'

12 'PostScript fonts are rendered by Adobe Type Manager (ATM), which is very intelligent software and does a very good job. So the fonts can be pretty dumb and it will still look very good on screen.'

13 'On the Macintosh you can always add some bitmaps of fonts if you have some critical small sizes, 10- or 12-point, and the font will also look good in small sizes.'

14 'The technology behind TrueType is a bit different. The rasterizer, which is built into the operating system, is very dumb. Because of this, you have to put all the intelligence into the fonts. You have to tell each character for each size how it's going to be displayed.'

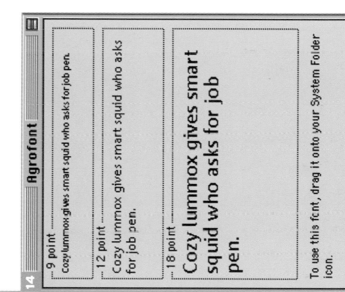

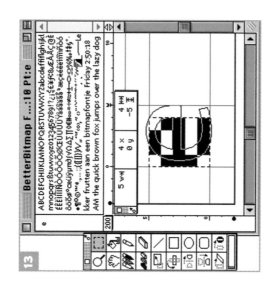

'UNFORTUNATELY THE DESIGN PROCESS IS A VERY SMALL PART OF SUCH A BIG JOB. IT'S THE BEST PART, OF COURSE, THE MOST FUN, BUT IN FONT DESIGN THERE'S SUCH AN IMMENSE AMOUNT OF TECHNICAL STUFF AND IMPLEMENTING STUFF.'

Techniques

De Groot had to take a PostScript font and make it work as a TrueType font. 'Making a PostScript font that works well for print is something I'm experienced in, and I know my tools very well. I use a lot of tools and when I design a font I can concentrate on designing the font and not be bothered too much by technical stuff. But the ministry's PCs use TrueType fonts, which can be rendered by the system, and you cannot add bitmap fonts to a TrueType font.' The process works kind of horribly, also, because you have to "hint" the characters, make bumps in them, adding instructions to the characters on how they'll display. For example, in 10-point this character gets a bump here so it displays a pixel less in this corner.' The hinting process alone took him two years.

De Groot used a piece of Russian software that, at $300, costs a fraction of licensing that the Western software costs, but does more or less the same tasks. However, he says, 'This 3.0 version was kind of in a beta stage, so I had to solve a lot of problems that were inherent in the version of the software I used. Unfortunately the design process is a very small part of such a big job. It's the best part, of course, the most fun, but in font design there's such an immense amount of technical stuff and implementing stuff.'

15

15 'Things like kerning are not the most exciting job but it really must be done and it takes a lot of time to do a good kerning table. And I always make kerning tables for all the European languages that can be set with a font.'

16 This image shows the proportions of cap height, x height, ascender and descender.

17 'In many display sizes Agrofont is better than Arial, because it's an open font: the lowercase e, c and s are very open. If you look at an Arial font, it is very closed, especially e, c and s. These closed characters don't work as well in small sizes. This is true not only for small sizes on screen but also generally, for example if you drive at night and read characters on a road sign. The same is true if you have closed characters like Helvetica or Arial – it's less readable in small sizes than more open characters like Frutiger and Agrofont.'

Arial abcdefghijklmnopqrstuvwxyz

Agro abcdefghijklmnopqrstuvwxyz

20 Maarten designed a metallic binder for four different kinds of information, the contents of which, he says, were specific to the various departments. 'The first part was to inspire people to use the new identity, make people aware.' The other parts were 'much more technical: the scalable structure, sizes, how to use the new typeface and logo, what Pantone colours to use, how to use the smaller, departmental logos.'

21 Booklets contained within the binder designed by Studio Dunbar.

22 'The design part was really modifying curves, and getting tension all over the font. Tension is how the inner curve relates to the outer curve. I tend to put a bit more diagonal contrast into the fonts. Even in a very neutral, sanserif font like this, it brings a bit of a humanistic, calligraphic touch. Much, much more subtle here than in Thesis, it's almost invisible here.'

18 'I want to change something on the italics. The ministry wanted to have numbers to set tables with, so all the widths of all the numbers in all the fonts had to be the same – the italic numbers had to be the same width as the plain and as the bold numbers. When I re-release it I want to make it a bit narrower, because it looks more elegant.'

19 'Freehand does live interpolation – you can draw a light character on screen and a black character on screen and you can interpolate a few steps in between. Live interpolation is kind of like the "blend" feature in Illustrator, but in Freehand it's much better because it's live – if you change something on one extreme, the things in the middle move as well, so you can design a normal weight without even touching it, just by modifying the black and the light.'

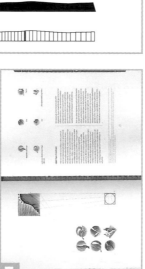

22

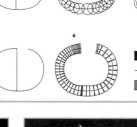

20

21

18

AgroSans-light 7:02:29 AM, lekker licht alweer
AgroSans-light italic abdpqhmnueœeffflyßig
ACROSANS-LIGHT SMALL CAPS OEF ZO EDEL

AgroSans-regular Normaal standaard gewoon
AgroSans-regular italic hé, spuitscheet plof
AGROSANS-REGULAR SMALL CAPS LUCHTIG

AgroSans-bold Nou ja? Een beetje dan 9.15
AgroSans-bold italic ha een schuine mop
AGROSANS-BOLD SMALL CAPS KLEINKAPS

AgroSans-heavy No kerning yet Poepertje
AGROSANS-HEAVY SMALL CAPS RUTSEFUT

AgroSans-black Een eerste testje 123456
AGROSANS-BLACK SMALL CAPS 789 DEF

19

ABCDEFGHIJKLMNOPQRSTUVWXYZ?&¢£$
abcdefghijklmnopqrstuvwxyz1234567890
ABCDEFGHIJKLMNOPQRSTUVWXYZ?&¢£$
abcdefghijklmnopqrstuvwxyz1234567890
ABCDEFGHIJKLMNOPQRSTUVWXYZ?&¢£$
abcdefghijklmnopqrstuvwxyz1234567890
ABCDEFGHIJKLMNOPQRSTUVWXYZ?&¢£$
abcdefghijklmnopqrstuvwxyz1234567890

'I DID A LOT OF WORK IN FREEHAND. AT THE BEGINNING OF THE DESIGN PROCESS, FREEHAND IS GOOD BECAUSE YOU CAN HAVE JUST A FEW MAIN CHARACTERS ON-SCREEN IN THREE WEIGHTS, AND YOU CAN DO THE BASIC DESIGN AND THEN GO ON TO A FONTS PROGRAM.'

CREDITS

Typography: Luc(as) de Groot
Manual design: Maarten Jurriaanse,
Studio Dunbar, 1998 for the Dutch Ministry of Agriculture, Nature Management and Fishery.
The metallic binder was printed by Emas BV, and the booklets inside by Ando BV.

DETAILS

Studio Dunbar
Bankaplein 1
2585 EV Den Haag
The Netherlands
tel: +31 70 416 7416
fax: +31 7C 416 7417
e-mail: studio@cumbar.nl
http://www.studiodunbar.com/

Luc(as) de Groot
FontFabrik
Apostel-Paulus-Straße 32
D-10823 Berlin, Germany
tel: +49 30 7870 3097
fax: +49 30 7870 5878
e-mail: type@fontfabrik.com
http://www.fontfabrik.com/

HARDWARE/SOFTWARE

Design work: PowerMac 8500 144Mb RAM, FontStudio 2.0, Macromedia Freehand 7.
Hinting & kerning work: Pentium II 266Mhz, FontLab 3.0, Manual, QuarkXPress, Illustrator and Photoshop on a Power Mac.

'WE KNOW SOME OTHER DIRECTORS WHO CAN'T EXPERIMENT TO THE LEVEL OF VISUALISATION WE CAN BECAUSE THEY DON'T HAVE THE KIT, AND IT MUST BE HUGELY FRUSTRATING. IT'S ABOUT HAVING A POWERFUL ENOUGH KIT TO REALISE YOUR OWN IDEAS.'

Biography

It's arguable, but many people in the design industry would agree that some of the most original and inventive TV graphics and ident work is originating from the computers of young designers in Britain, and a recent addition to this exciting new wave is London design duo Felt, a creative partnership between Dominic Bridges and Richard Carroll. Bridges had previously worked for TV identity specialist English & Pockett and Carroll was an independent graphic designer. Together as Felt, the past two years has seen them produce work through large ad agencies such as HHCL for ITV and TBWA London & Paris for Nissan, but they have also enjoyed creative freedom for smaller clients including Jameson's Whiskey and the Cruush juice bar chain. Bridges and Carroll originate their own photography, typefaces and animations, shoot 16mm and 35mm film and digital video, create their own sound design and edit themselves. Carroll explains: 'We both enjoy having an input into what we are doing. We recently directed our first commercial, on which we also did the animation and sound design.' They are currently directing commercials and music promos through a production company, Tsunami Films. 'We'd like to head more into commercials,' Bridges remarks, 'but we're also keen to keep on with our own kind of work and maybe head towards making some feature-length things.' 'If someone were to give us a script,' adds Carroll, 'that'd be great, but we've got quite a few of our own ideas as well. We're quite excited by things.'

Project

Spirit is a short video piece created by Bridges and Carroll in response to a visit to the Indonesian island of Sumatra. Carroll was returning from another commission when a chance encounter at an airport led Felt to be invited to make a documentary covering a workshop being held on Sumatra by an international forestry research organisation. As Carroll explains: 'The purpose of the workshop was to create software to enable people to plan sustainable development programmes. While we were there we picked up on the atmosphere around us, the environment, the people, the country and the politics a little bit as well and thought we'd make this piece, Spirit, as our comment on it.' To cover the workshop, Bridges and Carroll were using miniDV cameras, a prosumer digital video format and MiniDisc for sound recording. To capture the kind of material they wanted for Spirit they augmented this with stills cameras, Super 8 and 35mm film.

Development

'We took time out from the workshop to film the images in Spirit,' Carroll explains. 'They are from areas all over the country. We did a long field trip one morning – got up at 4am and drove across the island, about 400 miles, and we looked around a model village set up along the principals they were trying to establish in the software. It was like nirvana, you went over this hill and entered an idyllic lush valley with buffalo grazing. Some of the images are from this village, others are taken from buses, from moving cars and around certain towns.' 'We also spent a couple of nights in the rain forest itself camping out,' Bridges adds, 'which was quite a surreal experience, just trying to pick up on some of that vibe. We were there with two biologists who were interesting – they had a tendency to rip bark off trees and find the biggest scorpions or tarantulas and say "look at this guys!" and we'd be shitting ourselves!'

1 'We got loads of stuff we shot in Sumatra,' says Richard, 'we might include them in a photographic portfolio. The colour image of the couple was never used in the final film, but it feels close to how we felt the final vibe would be.' The image of the young girl was taken in the model village Dominic and Richard visited and was used in Spirit.

2 Frames made as tests for the dense textual 'mad phase', as Richard describes it, in Spirit.

3 One of the earliest test shots of type on acetate. The circles are formed by a swinging light bulb behind the acetate.

COMFORTABLE

NO ONE

CONFIDENCE

BELIEVER IN FATE

E HAS A MORE

FORTABLE LIFE, WO

ENCE THAN A

ER IN FATE

A MORE COMFORTABLE LIFE, WORRY FREE SOUL AND STRONGER CONF

Spirit runs at two and a half minutes. It took ten days to shoot and was edited, alongside other commissions, over a period of six weeks. Bridges and Carroll condensed all the sound, footage and images collected into a lyrical synthesis of their impressions of Sumatra. Slow, blurred and treated stills and shots of landscapes and people dissolve into each other to make a conceptual journey through a tropical landscape and foreign culture. Layered over the pictures, type pans, zooms and fades in and out, eventually spelling out in a kaleidoscopic crescendo of words and images the phrase 'No one has a more comfortable life and carefree soul than a believer in fate'. Carroll explains: 'We edited the footage first and worked on the type over that. The quote is from the Koran – Muslim religion is very strong in Sumatra. But I guess what it's all about is fate, they haven't got anything because they're quite a poor people but they were so happy. We hadn't decided on the quotation before we shot the footage, but we had in mind that we wanted to hook on to this religious aspect and the mundane day-to-day fatalistic way of looking at things. I guess the two went hand in hand once

we were back with the fresh impression of having just been there. We tried to construct a narrative from the image edit with the quote in the back of our minds. The type worked happily with the images once we had selected them. There are a few different levels of narrative in there, it's the narrative thing that interests us. Technically we know we can create interesting images – that's been proved through our various past commissions.' The soundtrack on Spirit was also engineered and edited by Bridges and Carroll, with treated samples of wildtrack recorded on MiniDisc in Sumatra.

Bridges and Carroll edited Spirit on a Media 100 non-linear edit suite already owned by Felt. 'There's a lot of stigma attached to the fact that you haven't shot live action before and so you don't tend to get that sort of work, so how are you supposed to go about getting it?' says Carroll. 'We bought a machine that could run the best quality software to do the kind of work we wanted to do. It was a way of getting a slick show-reel together to convince a production company to sign us, but having everything in-house also gives us huge freedom – it has the advantage of allowing us to experiment and realise ideas fully,' he adds.

4

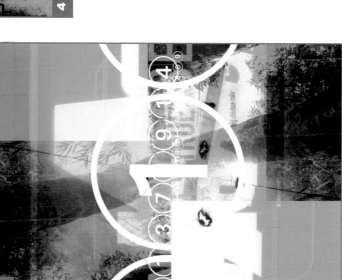

4 'The actual quote in the final film is different to the stills. These pictures were about getting our heads around what sort of fonts we would use and what sort of look it would have,' says Carroll.

4

'A LOT OF OUR WORK IS MULTI-LAYERED AND MULTI-IMAGE BASED, AND WE SHOOT WITH A LOT OF POST-PRODUCTION IN MIND SO WE CAN GRAB IMAGES ON STILLS CAMERAS OR SCANS OR SHOOT ON DV, 35MM OR WHATEVER. THERE ARE A LOT OF SPEED OR GRAIN CHANGES BUT THAT'S REALLY OUR STYLE, IT'S ALL INTEGRATED ANYWAY FOR A COMPLETELY DIFFERENT END RESULT.'

Technique

Type has to be handled differently in video compared to print or the web. The video frame is a fixed size no matter what the screen size is; for standard 4:3 aspect ratios it's 768x576 pixels for European PAL and 640x480 for NTSC. To avoid pixellation on any zooms, type is created larger than the frame size. The technical nature of video can make small, ornamental or serif type illegible or unbalanced – holes fill in and the serifs block out, so typefaces need to be carefully chosen. Unlike the printed page or web page, the edges of a video frame are not fixed and any type ranged top, bottom, left or right can disappear off the screen when viewed on a TV, so title-safe areas are usually adhered to. Generally when rasterising vector type or graphics points translate directly to pixels.

5

5

5 Sixteen frames taken from the final film version of Spirit, which screened at the ICA London in May 1999 and toured the UK as part of the OneDotZero digital film festival. The four typefaces are Handle Gothic, Aksidenz Grotesk, Lunatix and Epcom, a font created by Felt (right).

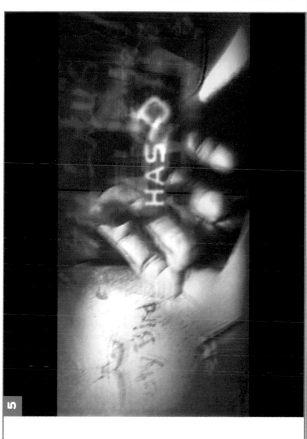

The layering and animation work on Spirit was done in Adobe's AfterEffects, which has become a film and TV industry standard for compositing work. It's been described as Photoshop for video and it works in a similar way. Elements are imported into layers and all aspects of their properties can be treated with filters and adjusted over a timeline to create visually rich sequences. Transparency is controlled through alpha channels or clipping paths in exactly the same way as Photoshop. The type was originated in Freehand 7 using just four typefaces; Handle Gothic, Aksidenz Grotesk, Lunatix and Epcom, a font created by Felt. Various weights, kerning and spacing were experimented with. 'We just chose the faces because they looked right and fitted the word, it was all very visually led,' says Carroll. Test pictures were made in Photoshop, and the duo experimented with blending layers of type and images prior to the final animated compositing in AfterEffects. 'Some of the type was imported directly into AfterEffects, animated and treated with filters. Other type was printed on to sheets of acetate which were then treated in numerous ways, some burnt with a blow torch, covered with glycerine or just back-lit by moving lights. They were then filmed by hand-held miniDV cameras, digitised into the Media 100 and superimposed in AfterEffects. This was to create real and random effects, avoiding the sterile predictable look of digital filters,' says Bridges, adding, 'You can't get anything out of Photoshop or AfterEffects unless you put something in!' The final result is a subtle, organic and ethereal look to the quality of the blended images that perfectly complements the subject matter.

HARDWARE/SOFTWARE

Adobe AfterEffects 4 with production bundle and ICE board, Adobe Photoshop 4 and 5 – 'The type control in 5 is pretty crap compared to 4,' says Carroll. Macromedia Freehand 7, Adobe Illustrator 5, Media 100, based on G3 Apple Mac, with 200Gb hard drive storage, Apple Powerbook G3 350, two Sony 3CCD miniDV cameras, scanner, Super 8 camera, 16mm camera, 35mm camera, stills camera, blow torch.

DETAILS

Felt can be contacted by e-mail: felt.london@dial.pipex.com

'I THINK TYPE IS THE PRIMARY EXPRESSIVE TOOL OF THE
GRAPHIC DESIGNER. THERE ARE TREMENDOUS
OPPORTUNITIES TO LET TYPOGRAPHIC FORMS ENTER
INTO THE DIALOGUE OF THE DESIGNED PIECE. IT IS MUCH
MORE THAN CHOOSING A TYPEFACE, IT IS CONSIDERING
TYPE AS A MALLEABLE AND EVER-CHANGING OBJECT.'

Biography

In 1996, San Francisco publisher Dan Rolleri decided to launch a new magazine which would capitalise on the success of such alternative lifestyle magazines such as *Bikini* and *RayGun*. With David Carson at the design helm, these two publications had pushed the boundaries of editorial design – with unqualified success. Rolleri envisioned something that content-wise could be even more wide ranging and far reaching. That new magazine was *Speak*, a magazine of popular culture, literature, music and art, and to art direct it, Rolleri brought in San Francisco-based Martin Venezky, a graphic designer whose company Appetite Engineers numbers everyone from Reebok and Warner Brothers to the San Francisco AIDS Foundation among its clients. Venezky's work has appeared in *Eye*, *Emigre* and *Graphis*, and he was recently listed among *I.D.* magazine's ID40 list of influential designers. While *Speak* has its own distinct identity, it always looks fresh, an achievement which is probably due to Venezky's habit of experimenting with anything and everything in his sumptuous, multi-layered and multi-textured design work, discovering inspiration in the found object and the chance encounters of his daily experience. For example, for last April/May's issue of *Speak*, he utilised old wood type to create headlines for an article on a book fair in Guadalajara, Mexico.

Last year American book publisher Chronicle Books asked Venezky to design a book of photography and writings by David Perry and Barry Gifford. 'David had been introduced to Barry when Barry wrote a short story for his first book of photos, *Hot Rod*. They decided to do a bigger project together, and approached Chronicle with the idea of documenting a journey along the US/Mexico border. Chronicle agreed and off they

went,' explains Venezky of the subsequent book, *Bordertown*. Photographer David Perry describes the book as 'a raw and immediate visual and literary response to a ribbon of land along the Mexican American border. Part photo album, part scrapbook, it is a collage of imagery and imagination, fiction and non-fiction, real and surreal, the sacred and profane.'

Venezky's relationship with Perry began when he designed *Hot Rod* for the photographer. 'We became friends, and he contributed several photo stories to *Speak* magazine. When the *Bordertown* project happened, David asked Chronicle if I could design the book. Michael Carabetta (Chronicle's senior art director) and Caroline Herter (the book's editor) invited me to Chronicle to discuss the project, and I was subsequently hired. I then brought Geoff Kaplan into the project, at first to help collect material, and later to help organise and design the book,' recalls Venezky. Kaplan, a fellow alumni of Cranbrook School of Art, had met Venezky when he sent him one of his typefaces to use in the first issue of *Speak*. 'We stayed in touch and after he graduated, I invited him to help with *Bordertown*. We have collaborated on several other projects since then,' says Venezky.

'The book's premise was unusual, and writers and photographers do not usually collaborate so closely,' he continues. 'After looking over the material David and Barry brought back from the journey, Michael and Caroline thought that the book should be designed like no other. I was asked to pretty much invent a new form that would fit the experience. And they were open to whatever I thought would be best. Imagine how much pressure that brings!'

Initial approach and development

Even before Perry and Gifford undertook their trip, Perry began to think about the book's design: 'Instead of a chronological order, I chose an order of pictures that would visually carry the viewer across the border into a typical bordertown; past the rush of people, the beggars, peddlers, curios and signs; day eventually turning into night and putting you in the heart of darkness.' They returned with 'a mountain of material, handed it to Martin and basically said "make it a book!" I had complete trust in him as an artist,' enthuses Perry.

Venezky picks up the story: 'David had already printed up his favourite pictures and had placed them in a casual order that gave them a logical sequence. We read the manuscript before we did anything else. It wasn't even edited yet. We were also given photocopies of Barry's notebook, which we studied page by page.'

'After studying the material we began collecting things that related to it – originally just to have them around us as inspiration. In this particular case, that meant our travelling throughout Latin parts of San Francisco and Los Angeles, and later to Tijuana in Mexico for material we couldn't get in the US,' continues Venezky. 'Only when we visited Tijuana did we really understand what bordertowns were like. How everything hits you at once. Everyone is trying to capture your attention (and your money). It is very hectic and confusing, especially if you don't speak Spanish – which neither Geoff nor I do. That became a central point of the book's design. Also, the collision between old and new, fantasy and reality, religion and profanity all became important forces in the design,' he explains.

1 A selection of the original items collected by Venezky and Kaplan in Mexico. The flower motif, waving Pico peanut and Tu Destino (written on the soap box) are used throughout the book, as the spreads show. Venezky says the Mexican and border imagery "in some ways comment on the photographs and articles that David and Barry brought back. Other times they work almost by defacing the "precious" quality of the artwork and literature. The mix of vernacular and art within the book adds a layer of conflict. It also brought a graphic abstraction that helps tie the elements together.'

2 The 'E' and the 'N' of 'El Mexicano' is used in the word 'Bordertown' on the book's cover.

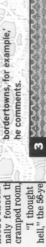

3 Venezky didn't restrict his material to graphic elements, as these spreads from the book *Bordertown* show. Mexican lace and wedding dress fabrics (below) were used as background texture. The point of collecting the material was originally for inspiration, but then Venezky decided he'd like to use it in the book's design. 'We wanted to gain a better understanding of the material, but we didn't want to become "experts" on the region. Therefore our research was done through observation, interaction and collecting, rather than studying histories of bordertowns, for example,' he comments.

Whilst collecting the material, Venezky had no idea how Chronicle would react to the idea of contributing his own elements to the book. 'It's unusual for designers to bring in their own images and material. Usually we are just asked to shape other peoples' material and to stay out of the way. But when Michael and Caroline encouraged us, we were delighted and collected even more earnestly,' he recalls. Perry also positively encouraged the approach: 'Because of our past history, Martin knows where I'm coming from, and we worked very closely together on this. I wanted his design to effect the book, which is why I suggested him to Chronicle in the first place,' he explains. 'David agreed that, although the design might weaken some of the photos, the technique would strengthen the book as a whole. What an enlightened position for a photographer to take!' adds Venezky.

4

Scanning and cataloguing all the material collected in Mexico, Venezky and Kaplan were then able to start formulating the design of the book. Through enlarging elements, they were able to isolate the characters they wanted to use.

CASA LUCAS
$3.19

V◆DA

TU DESTINO

It was during their travels that Venezky and Kaplan began to develop ideas. 'The travelling and collecting happen before any ideas are formed. As we experience things, all kinds of ideas start to form,' asserts Venezky. 'On returning, he and Kaplan gave a first presentation that showed a range of potential page layouts: 'From very quiet and reserved to extremely loud. We expected the publisher to choose something in the middle. But they liked the entire range,' says Venezky. 'Whenever we asked permission to try one thing or another, Caroline always answered with "Whatever you think is best." Wow! After that, we worked on our own, planning out the book and creating all the design. Our next presentation was the first galley of the entire book. After we had scanned all the articles and photos and mapped out the basic rhythm, Geoff and I actually designed the entire book in three extremely long days!' he adds.

'I HAD TO BE CAREFUL NOT TO "PRE-DESIGN" THE BOOK IN MY HEAD. I ALWAYS START BY DEVELOPING A PROCESS OR STRATEGY AND THEN LET THAT PROCESS TAKE ITS COURSE. ALTHOUGH THAT PROCESS WORKS WELL FOR ME, I HAD ALMOST ALWAYS USED IT FOR SPEAK, NEVER FOR A LARGE BOOK PROJECT LIKE THIS. SO, I HAVE TO ADMIT, I WAS A LITTLE AFRAID THAT NOTHING WOULD COME OUT OF IT.'

Technique

Having assembled a wealth of materials, Venezky began by scanning everything. 'Perry's photos were scanned low-resolution for placement and then scanned as duotones by the printer/prepress operators. All the newspaper articles that Barry provided were scanned partly as line art and partly as greyscale to get the best reproduction. All the fabric swatches were photocopied, then scanned at high resolution. All the line art was photocopied then scanned. We didn't do any manipulation at all. We had all the scanned artwork printed out and catalogued in a notebook for easy reference.'

Having scanned, printed out and catalogued all the artwork, Venezky and Kaplan began to design the book. 'We sat side-by-side for three days in front of the computer. The book was designed in QuarkXPress on a Macintosh. We used a Hewlett-Packard scanner and a Canon photocopier. We used Adobe Photoshop to clean up our scans,' Venezky explains. 'As you can imagine, the production took a very long time. Each image had to be sized and placed exactly at high-resolution. Very painstaking work,' he adds.

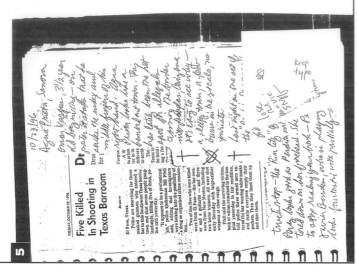

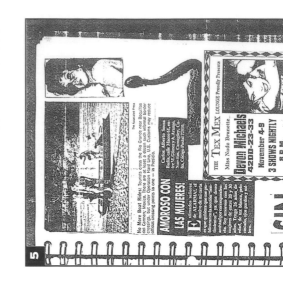

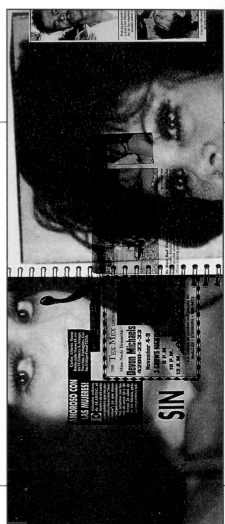

Most of Gifford's manuscript for the book was handwritten in a collection of notebooks. 'We photocopied many versions of the manuscript. In a way, it helps remind people of the collection process, that this was written "on the run". It also had a nice rhythm which worked well with other rhythms and patterns throughout the book,' explains Venezky.

'Some of the original thoughts involved reproducing all of Barry's handwriting as the main text of the book. We thought that it would be too hard to read, but agreed to keep portions of Barry's handwriting to remind the reader that Barry and David were travelling as tourists,' says Venezky.

'MOST OF THE TEXT IS SET IN KABEL AND SCOTCH ROMAN. WE HAD SEEN A SIMILAR COMBINATION IN AN OLD ROAD ATLAS, AND LIKED THE FEELING IT GAVE – A DELICACY AND STRENGTH THAT WAS VERY APPEALING. I LIKED THE COMBINATION SO MUCH THAT I CONTINUE TO USE IT ON MY STATIONERY AND LETTERWRITING AND PROMOTIONAL MATERIALS.'

While there were advantages to inputting everything into the computer before the design was created – 'for example, it was useful in allowing us to try lots of different combinations of elements quickly' – Venezky did not want the book to look like a computer-generated project: 'The language of the computer really has nothing to do with the content, so we went to great lengths to keep it from determining how things looked. We were constantly trying to make the computer irregular and imprecise. To shift things, break things, knock things into each other. The computer is awfully resistant to this kind of thing!' he laughs.

'The computer allowed us to combine elements quickly, but we developed the creative sense of the book independently of the computer. And although I didn't know it from the start, the book became a genuine collaboration not only between writer and photographer, but between authors and designers. It was one of those rare projects where all of our skills were tested and all of our thoughts respected. Creating and producing this book was unlike any other project I have worked on,' concludes Venezky.

7 Along with observations, Gifford wrote a number of fictional passages for the book, including this one. 'We decided to keep all of them completely stark as a counterpoint to the rest of the book. We thought that these sections were like dreams or meditations. The reader can "sleep" through them and blot out all the noise of the world. Then the short story is over and we return to the shouting again,' explains Venezky.

8 Perry's photography style throughout the trip was to 'photograph in a fast and loose street style; and be as incognito as two big gringos could be. I'd use available light, use my Nikons and my point & shoot - take landscapes, portraits, details; whatever caught my eye. Include everything in the picture.' He was closely involved with the book's design: 'Martin and I would discuss cropping and picture placement, how far we could overlay type on pictures without compromising the photograph, printing to compensate for the metallic inks, those kinds of things,' he says.

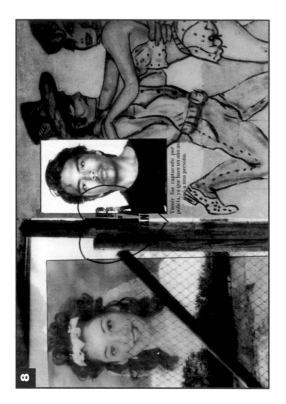

9 Venezky and Kaplan collected a range of posters from which they could lift details, as seen here. The book uses just three inks, black, brown and silver: 'We chose a colour related to the earth (brown) and one related to the heavens (silver). The sacred and profane. The harsh reality of everyday life, and the gilded faith of religion. I chose these colours before we even knew what we were going to do with them. I just knew they were right,' says Venezky.

'I DON'T THINK PHOTOGRAPHS HAVE TO HAVE A PRECIOUS WHITE BORDER TO BE POWERFUL. ALSO, AN IMPORTANT THOUGHT, WE WANTED THE BOOK TO BE ORIGINAL; TO CREATE A NEW FORM OF BOOK. IN ORDER FOR THAT TO HAPPEN, BARRY AND I HAD TO GIVE UP PRECONCEIVED NOTIONS OF HOW A BOOK IS SUPPOSED TO LOOK.' DAVID PERRY, PHOTOGRAPHER

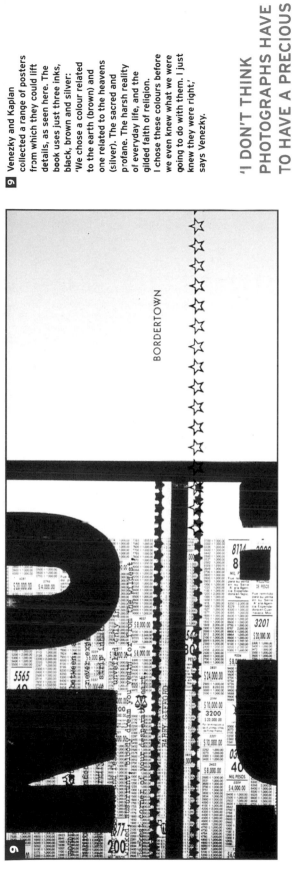

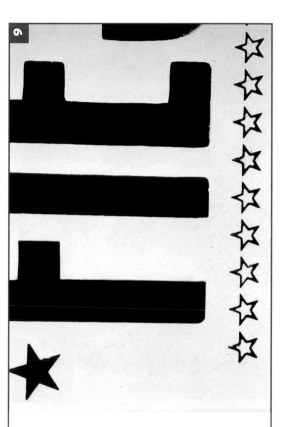

HARDWARE/SOFTWARE
QuarkXPress, Adobe Photoshop, Macintosh computer, Hewlett-Packard scanner, Canon photocopier.

DETAILS
Martin Venezky, Appetite Engineers
4503 18th Street
San Francisco, CA 94114
USA
tel: + 1 415 252 8122
fax: +1 415 252 8142
e-mail: venezky@sirius.com
website: www.appetiteengineers.com

David Perry
e-mail: kdperry@pacbell.net
website: www.davidperrystudio.com
emagazine: tijuanataxi.net

Biography

Film title design once could boast just one household name, Saul Bass, who, to ensure that his stunning graphic interpretations of Hitchcock movies were seen in their entirety, famously used to sneak into movie theatres and make sure that the house lights went down *before* the titles started and stayed down until that last 'Made in Cinemascope' had rolled off the screen. But this decade has seen a real resurgence in film title design, and it's not just due to bigger budgets and technological wizardry; last year's strikingly original titles for 'Elizabeth', created by Malcolm Garratt and the AMX Digital Studio in London, were worked up and produced entirely on the Apple Mac.

When it comes to similarly inventive and original sequences, many of America's best film-makers turn to one company, Balsmeyer & Everett. Mimi Everett and Randy Balsmeyer began working together in 1979 in Seattle, at Alpha Cine FX; Mimi in optical layout, Randy in design and animation. In 1980 they moved to New York to work for one of the world's top film title studios, R/Greenberg Associates, until 1985. 'Prior to our working together, I received a BFA in design from CalArts, and was a principal in Brown Cow Graphics in Spokane, WA. Mimi went to school at Sarah Lawrence College and the University of Washington, where she studied documentary film-making,' recalls Balsmeyer. 'I accidentally got into title design for films when my interests in graphic design, typography, photography and computers all converged in the area of graphic animation,' he adds.

At R/GA, Randy's skills expanded to include direction and cinematography, until in 1986 he and Mimi decided to start their own company (and family – in true Hollywood happy-ending style, Balsmeyer and Everett were married in 1991 and now have two young daughters). 'We've kept our company intentionally small, with a permanent staff of about ten, including graphic designers, editors and CGI artists for 3D animation and 2D compositing. Although each person here has his or her own personal specialities, everyone has to be a bit of a generalist. We have a motion control/insert stage, and a bunch of SGI and Macintosh computers. We also do our own digital film recording,' explains Balsmeyer. The duo count among their clients auteurs such as Robert Altman, Spike Lee, Hal Hartley, David Cronenberg, the Coen Brothers and Jim Jarmusch, who has used them on all his films since their initial collaboration on 1991's 'Night on Earth', right through tc this year's 'Ghost Doç: The Way of the Samurai'. 'On the film "Night on Earth", we came up with a fairly elaborate sequence involving motion control photography of two globes, with smoke and clouds. The sequence was inspired by Tom Waits' title track, and was intended to feel like a drunken astronaut's return to earth. We also came up with the wall of clocks which separated the film's five simultaneous components, each set in a different city,' explains Balsmeyer. 'Our working relationship with Jim is very good. He is alternately inspired and funny, then moody and depressed. The key to our joint success seems to be a mutual level of trust - that each of us is trying to do the right thing for the good of the film,' he says of working with the film-maker.

'I'VE FOUND THAT MY BEST IDEAS HAPPEN WHEN I'M NOT TRYING TO FORCE THEM. SOMETIMES A WALK DOWN THE STREET IS THE BEST SOURCE. I TRY TO JUST KEEP MY EYES OPEN AND LOOK FOR THINGS THAT MAKE ME SMILE. I TRY FOR THE MOST PART NOT TO STEAL FROM OTHER ART AND DESIGN IMAGES, ALTHOUGH OCCASIONALLY I'LL WANT TO MAKE IMAGES THAT FEEL CONNECTED TO A PARTICULAR STYLE OR PERIOD.'

YEAR OF THE HORSE

1

Background and initial approach

'In the past, Jim (Jarmusch) has kept his titles separate from the body of the film, and has frequently used fades-to-black to separate scenes. For "Ghost Dog" he wanted to try something new. In the interest of getting the story started quickly, he wanted to try titles over picture,' explains Balsmeyer. 'The first time we meet Ghost Dog (played by Forest Whitaker), a Samurai hit-man, he is alone reading a book called *Hagakure: The Book of the Samurai*. Because it's important to the narrative, Jim wanted to use text from this book to connect different scenes. My job essentially was to make all these text elements look and feel right for the picture.'

1 The design of the titles for 'Ghost Dog' grew out of Balsmeyer & Everett's experience on the titles for 'Year of the Horse', Jarmusch's documentary about Neil Young and Crazy Horse, which in turn came out of their collaboration on 'Dead Man'. 'You know, one thing just leads to another,' laughs Balsmeyer. 'Jim had admired some of Neil's hand-lettered album notes and wanted to get that look and feel into the titles for the film. We began with a great hand-lettered font, FF Erikrighthand, which was designed by Erik van Blokland for FontFont. We brought it into Fontographer, changed its weight and width, and created the title animation,' he explains.

'I THINK THAT A GREAT TITLE SEQUENCE DOES TWO THINGS. FIRST, TO BE GOOD, IT MUST SET UP THE FILM IN THE MOST CONCENTRATED WAY POSSIBLE. BY CONCENTRATED, I MEAN THAT SOME ESSENCE OF THE FILM IS DISTILLED INTO THE SIMPLEST, MOST POWERFUL VISUAL FORM. SECOND, AND THIS IS WHAT ELEVATES IT TO GREAT, IT MUST BE A SELF-CONTAINED VISUAL THOUGHT, SO THAT EVEN WHEN VIEWED BY ITSELF IT FEELS COMPLETE, AND IS MEMORABLE AS A DISTINCT ENTITY.'

Development, working process and techniques

For 'Ghost Dog', Jarmusch wanted to take the hand-lettering idea even further: and editor Jay Rabinowitz encouraged him to use his own handwriting. 'Rather than just writing out the credits himself, he wanted us to be able to design and manipulate the lettering, so we tried two different companies that create fonts from handwriting samples, Signature Software, Inc. and Alexander Walter,' says Balsmeyer.

The two different companies that create fonts from handwriting samples, Signature Software, Inc. and Alexander Walter, each use a different approach in sampling a person's handwriting. Signature Software asked Jarmusch to fill out a Personal Font and Handwriting Sample Form (below), while Alexander Walter required a lengthy bit of nonsense text, which is then selectively sampled. 'Both companies delivered excellent fonts in just a few days, and each had had accompanying "randomizer" software that would use alternate characters so that if a word had two Gs they would not be exactly the same shape.'

ABCDEFGHIJKLMNOPQRSTUVWXYZ
ABCDEFGHIJKLMNOPQRSTUVWXYZ
ABCDEFGHIJKLMNOPQRSTUVWXYZ
ABCDEFGHIJKLMNOPQRSTUVWXYZ
1234567890   1234567890
☆ + + +   1234567890   + + + ☆

— — — = + \ | ⸢ ⸤ ⸥ ⸣ ; : ' " , < . > / / ? ! · # $ ^ * ☆

( ) ( ) ( ) ( ) ( ) ( ) ( )
. ; : . ; " " (( ) , ; " " ? ! ? ! ? ! # # # * * * $ + + etc.

THE QUICK BROWN FOX JUMPS OVER THE LAZY DOG.
The quick brown fox jumps over the lazy dog. over over over over

A YELLOW HERTZ TAXICAB, NOT KHAKI, IS THE NORM.
A yellow hertz taxicab, not khaki, is the norm.

KHRUSHCHEV WILL OPENLY VANQUISH THE JUNTA IN IRAQ.
Khrushchev will openly vanquish the junta in Iraq.

A YOGA GURU WILL HEW THE YUCCA WITH A HACKSAW.
A yoga guru will hew the yucca with a hacksaw. hacksaw.

SIX DEAF NAVAJO REJECT STIFF TAX BILLS.
Six deaf navajo reject stiff tax bills.

THE KEYNOTE PHARAOH DID DROP A SHOE IN CUBA.
The keynote pharaoh did drop a shoe in Cuba.

THE COTTONWOOD CANOE HAS A HOTROD MOTOR AND ROOM FOR A
BROKE RABBI. The cottonwood canoe has a hotrod motor and room for a broke rabbi. for a broke rabbi. hotrod motor and...

You hope havoc and chaos will ebb when you tattoo a kiwi at a zoo. YOU HOPE HAVOC AND CHAOS WILL EBB WHEN YOU TATTOO A KIWI AT A ZOO.

THE SOMEWHAT WORTHWHILE OFFBEAT PROJECT EMPLOYS AN ELOQUENT ELOQUENT COWBOY. The somewhat worthwhile offbeat project employs an eloquent cowboy. ● IT IS A BIOGRAPHY AND BIBLIOGRAPHY BIBLIOGRAPHY of of A CLUBHOUSE JOBHOLDER WHO EATS OFFENSIVE GARBAGE TOXIC CABBAGE AND FROZEN CROCODILE MEAT, AND DRINKS BOOZE. It is a biography and bibliography of a clubhouse jobholder who eats offensive toxic cabbage and frozen crocodile meat, and drinks booze. LACK OF ALCOHOL PROHIBITION CAUSED BLUEBOOK COHESION FIBROSIS. Lack of alcohol prohibition caused bluebook cohesion fibrosis. HE MUST THEN ESCAPE A DOWNPOUR BY ENTERING THE WEATHER-PROOF WEATHERPROOF TOWNHOUSE. He must escape a downpour by entering the weatherproof townhouse. townhouse. townhouse. A SOJOURN IN AN ABOVEGROUND TURBOJET WHIRLPOOL ENDS WITH A DOZEN BUCKSHOT CROQUET BALLS. A sojourn in an aboveground turbojet whirlpool ends with a dozen buckshot croquet balls.

ABCDEFGHIJKLMNOPQRSTUVWXYZ
ABCDEFGHIJKLMNOPQRSTUVWXYZ

ATLANTA	CHICAGO	ERIE ERIE
GEORGIA	INDIANA	KANSAS
MEMPHIS	ORLANDO	KANSAS
SACRAMENTO	UTAH	QUEBEC
YELLOWSTONE		WISCONSIN
BOSTON	DALLAS	FARGO
HOUSTON	JACKSONVILLE	LEXINGTON
NASHVILLE	PITTSBURG	RENO
TEXAS	PITTSBURG	XENIA
ZANESVILLE	VIRGINIA	XENIA
	PITTSBURG	XENIA

Personal Font™
Handwriting Sample Form

Form 65411771   Form #5497

US Patent #5411771

Name: _____

DIRECTOR OF PHOTOGRAPHY
ROBBY MÜLLER

'THERE ARE OBVIOUSLY FASHIONS IN TITLE DESIGN, AND THE CURRENT TREND SEEMS TO BE TOWARDS EVER MORE DENSE AND LAYERED VISUAL EXTRAVAGANZAS. TO A LARGE EXTENT THIS HAS BEEN FOSTERED BY NEW COMPUTER TECHNOLOGY WHICH ALLOWS FOR UNLIMITED PLAY WITH TYPE AND IMAGES, WHICH WAS NEVER REALLY POSSIBLE IN THE DAYS OF PHOTO-MECHANICAL OPTICALS. UNFORTUNATELY, THIS IS SORT OF A SOLUTION-IN-SEARCH-OF-A-PROBLEM SCENARIO. FOR MYSELF, WHEN I BEGIN EACH NEW PROJECT, I TRY TO STAY TECHNIQUE-AGNOSTIC, LET THE IDEA BE THE DRIVING FORCE, AND THEN FIND THE APPROPRIATE TECHNIQUE TO REALISE IT.'

'Throughout the process Jim would sometimes be quite specific about what he had envisioned and in other instances he left it up to us to propose ideas. This is a great way to work, because he defines a general direction, and leaves it up to us to come up with the specifics of design', enthuses Balsmeyer. 'It is very much Jim's movie, so our goal was to understand his overall vision and make the graphics consistent with that, but as a collaboration rather than a client/vendor relationship,' he adds.

3 'we chose the font created by Alexander Walter entirely on the basis of the style of lettering Jim had submitted. This was brought into Fontographer, modified and the character set enlarged with things like ©, ü and ® to create a "Ghost Dog" font.'

'Jay (Rabinowitz, Jarmusch's editor) made several rough edits of the opening sequence on the Avid, before I even joined the project. In the middle of the title sequence the first two *Hagakure* quotes were to appear. But no matter how he cut the scene, the superimposed text felt intrusive,' recalls Balsmeyer. 'I suggested introducing the *Hagakure* text with close-up insert shots of a real book rather than supers, so that the scene would not feel interrupted. Jim liked the idea, so we made a still frame in Illustrator and Photoshop that Jay could use to edit in and see if the idea worked. It did, so we proceeded to make a real prop book and shot the inserts in our studio (Jim directing, me shooting),' he explains.

Balsmeyer and his team then moved on to the title sequence itself, the first half of which alternates shots of flying birds with (the bird's) aerial POVs. 'The bird shots seemed to want to be clean (no titles), and my first impression was that the credits should float in front of the aerial shots as if they were somewhere between the moving camera and the ground,' explains Balsmeyer. 'We took a cut of the scene, and Gray (Miller, a designer/editor at Balsmeyer & Everett) and I worked together to create our own version in AfterEffects (4.0) and Premiere (5.0). We used Beta SP as our tape format, both in and out.'

4 'The first time we meet Ghost Dog, he is alone reading a book called *Hagakure: The Book of the Samurai*. We created a prop book and shot two inserts for this first scene, to introduce the audience to the book's content'.

5 Throughout the body of the film, there are 14 occasions when text from *Hagakure* is superimposed over the background to bridge two scenes. In each case, Ghost Dog's crest appears at the bottom of the 'page'.

6 'For the *Hagakure* text, we began with a font called Calligraphic 421 (designed by Georg Trump). We chose this for its vaguely Asian/calligraphic style, even though it is a conventional roman (not italic) alphabet which looks plausible as a printed book page. Again, we brought it into Fontographer, and modified the punctuation marks, which seemed too large and elaborate for book printing. The resulting font was used both to create the prop book pages and the superimposed optical text. So, the goal of our involvement was to create two styles of text which were to be associated with an individual. The title graphics were tied to the film-maker, and the *Hagakure* pages were a connection to the Ghost Dog character,' says Balsmeyer.

4 The major difference between the book pages
5 and the optical supers was the leading. 'Whereas in the book pages Jim wanted to limit the amount of text seen on-screen, he wanted to fit a great deal of text into the supers, so we fussed a lot with the supered text, using letter-spacing, word-spacing, horizontal scaling and manual kerning to make each card

as nicely arranged as it could be (i.e. no widows or orphans, hung punctuation, etc.). The apparent difference in weight of the lettering is purely a by-product of the fact that on film, light "blooms". So on a dark field, near-white letters tend to look fatter, and dark letters on a light field (the book pages) tend to look thinner,' explains Balsmeyer.

4

earthquakes [...]
cliffs, dying of disease, or committing
seppuku at the death of one's master.
And every day without fail one should
consider himself as dead. This is the
substance of the Way of the Samurai.

5

Our bodies are given life from the midst of nothingness. Existing where there is nothing is the meaning of the phrase, "Form is emptiness." That all things are provided for by nothingness is the meaning of the phrase, "Emptiness is form." One should not think that these are two separate things.

6

The Way of the Samurai is found in death. Meditation on inevitable death should be performed daily. Every day when one's body and mind are at peace,

7

In the first half of the title sequence, each of the actors' names appears in an aerial shot and appears to 'fly' somewhere between the camera and the ground.

The "Ghost Dog" title is a good example of using alternate characters to avoid repeats (G and O), as is the writer/director frame, where the R also uses alternate characters. In the film itself, Forest Whitaker plays a "Samurai hit-man" and wears a jacket with a Japanese crest on it. We decided to integrate the crest into the main title to make it "his" crest,' explains Balsmeyer.

Although a lowercase of the font was created, Jarmusch did not want to use it in the opening credits as he thought it looked too childish, but approved its use in the end credits.

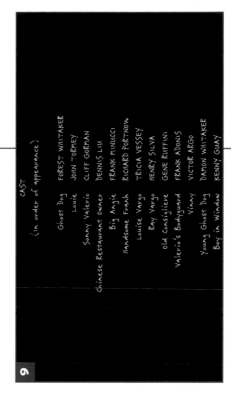

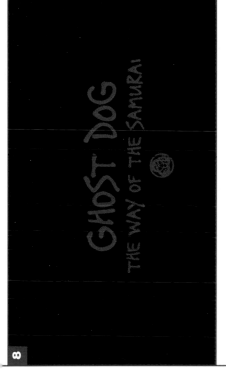

'The second half of the credits appear over a sequence of Ghost Dog walking through the town at night. Gray and I made a first pass at this section, placing the titles off-centre in the frame to best accommodate the background picture. But Jim felt that this placement was too active and distracted from the picture, so we centred the titles at the bottom of the frame, where they're more predictable and therefore less distracting,' says Balsmeyer.

'Once we had the font finalised (see captions), we produced all the main title art in Illustrator and the end titles in QuarkXPress. The main title layouts were e-mailed to Film Effects in Toronto, where the final opticals were completed. The key frame positions for the title animation were pulled as still frames from the AfterEffects project with a field chart superimposed, so that Film Effects could precisely match our video version. The end credits were output as Linotronic film negatives and shot conventionally on our animation camera.'

CAST
(In order of appearance)

Ghost Dog	FOREST WHITAKER
Louie	JOHN TORMEY
Sonny Valerio	CLIFF GORMAN
Chinese Restaurant owner	DENNIS LIU
Big Angie	FRANK MINUCCI
Handsome Frank	RICHARD PORTNOW
Louise Vargo	TRICIA VESSEY
Ray Vargo	HENRY SILVA
Old Consigliere	GENE RUFFINI
Valerio's Bodyguard	FRANK ADONIS
Vinny	VICTOR ARGO
Young Ghost Dog	DAMON WHITAKER
Boy in Window	KENNY GUAY

DETAILS
Balsmeyer & Everett
459 West 15th Street
NYC 10011
New York
USA
tel: +1 212 627 3430
fax: +1 212 989 6528
website: balsmeyer-everett.com

HARDWARE/SOFTWARE
Fontographer, Illustrator 8, QuarkXPress, AfterEffects 4.0, Premiere 5.0, Softimage, Cineon and Chalice. SGI workstations. 300Mgz Apple Mac. Truevision Targa 2000 RTX and 9Gb array.

CREDITS
GHOST DOG: THE WAY OF THE SAMURAI
Director: Jim Jarmusch
Director of Photography: Robby Müller
Editor: Jay Rabinowitz
© 1999 Plywood Productions, Inc.

TITLE SEQUENCE
Balsmeyer & Everett
Cinematography/Photography: Randy Balsmeyer
Designer/Editor: Gray Miller

Background

With the advent of desktop publishing a decade ago, the independent publishing sector suddenly came alive to design possibilities previously unavailable to the hundreds of sad black-and-white A4 fanzines covering everything from m-base jazz and ska music to the personal, political and cultural. A whole spate of new magazines was born which could be easily and cheaply produced by anyone with a Mac Classic running QuarkXPress, amongst them art and culture magazine *Frieze*. Still going strong eight years on, the pilot issue was published in the summer of 1991. It was then, as it is now, a British magazine with the broad remit of reporting and interpreting international contemporary art and culture. The magazine has always revolved around three key people; original editors Matthew Slotover and Tom Gidley (now credited as art director) and managing editor Amanda Sharp (now publisher). 'We tried to raise money in various ways – sponsorship, backers, whatever, but no one would give 22-year-olds money to do something which was very wordy', recalls Slotover.

Gordon Matta-Clark:
rocking the foundation

by Jeff Rian

The celebrated but under or unnoticed (like Bas Jan Ader) artist Gordon Matta, 1943, the son of surrealist painter Roberto Matta Echaurren, at the prestigious Parsons School of Architecture, mostly in New York, studied architecture and music at his Cornell School of Architecture. In 1971 he co-founded a restaurant called Food, where artists were a whole buildings. He became the corner of a whole buildings, he surveyed the suicide of his twin brother in 1976, and died less than two years later of a pancreatic cancer on August 27, 1978. His was a brief but intense life; his career cutting barely ten years.

'So we produced a pilot issue, which Tom designed, that was supposed to be a sampler really, but we commissioned original articles and put a cover price on it,' he continues. 'Most of the copies were sent for free to advertising agencies who mostly chucked them away, but we put a few copies into shops and they did really well. We printed 1,500 copies and everyone did everything for free and the printing only cost about £2,000. The whole thing was laid out on a computer using an early version of QuarkXPress. We were probably one of the first magazines to be entirely done on a Mac. We did it on a Mac Plus, which eventually blew up!'

'READERS, EDITORS AND DESIGNERS ALL KNOW THAT AN INGREDIENT OF A MAGAZINE'S SUCCESS WILL BE ITS DESIGN: THE DESIGN THAT TOUCHES OFF THAT INTANGIBLE FEELING OF RIGHTNESS, OF IDENTIFICATION IN THE READER BROWSING AT THE BOOKSTALL.'

DAVID HILLMAN, PENTAGRAM

As with all new ventures, critics attempted to pigeonhole *Frieze*, trying to associate it with various established groups and magazines. At about the time that *Frieze* launched, rival British arts magazine *Artscribe* was beginning to flag. *Frieze*, however, was a very different magazine in outlook and look to its now defunct rival.
'Everyone said "oh yeah great you're the new *Artscribe*", but we didn't think of ourselves like that at all,' complains Slotover. 'We've sometimes been associated with Goldsmiths College but it's only because we ran the very first interview with Damien Hirst and focused on other artists from there. It's been a positive thing and a negative thing. People will write us off because they don't like those artists – "doesn't Damien Hirst own that magazine" or they don't like the show-offy stuff. Actually there's only about one piece in each issue that is about young British art, but we will probably always have to live with those sort of misconceptions.'

Initial approach and development

In the first issue both Slotover and Gidley were credited as editors and art directors. 'We kind of changed that' says Slotover, 'after Amanda started in September 1991 as managing editor – but then we all became editors. We did all have this idea that we could all do everything to start with – but of course as you start to have more work to do it's just crazy to have everyone deciding everything. It was a lot of duplication and a waste of time – although the arguments can be quite fruitful. Eventually you begin to realise and learn each other's strengths and stop treading on each other's toes. It's much less loose than it originally was; now I'm basically the editor, Amanda is basically the publisher and Tom is basically the art director. Tom designs the layout for each issue and if anyone strongly objects they voice those objections and he takes it all on board.' Despite claiming to be just the editor, Slotover is very hands on and committed to all aspects of publishing *Frieze*, including its design and print.

1 Pilot issue. 'Without the Mac, *Frieze* would never have started – there's no question.' Explains Slotover: 'When we launched someone from *Artscribe* said "I don't know how you're managing," I said, "how much do you spend on typesetting each issue?" and he replied "£5,000". I said "we spend £500!" We only have two copies of the pilot left and I'd sell them for a £1,000 each, well maybe one of them!'

Don't look Now

The emerging feminist artists of the 90s have adopted a very different set of priorities and strategies than those of their immediate predecessors. Dan Cameron examines the situation in New York as reflected by two recent shows, while Anthony Iannacci interviews four young Italian artists.

1 frieze

pilot issue summer 1991 £3

CHRISTIAN BOLTANSKI CRITICAL DÉCOR ÉMIGRÉ ANGUS FAIRHURST GRAHAM GUSSIN DAMIEN HIRST ALBERT IRVIN ART & LANGUAGE A NEW INTERNATIONALISM AVI PRODUCTIONS ART IN RUINS

2 frieze

art & feminism
sophie calle
tatsuo miyajima
matt mullican
max vadukul
richard wentworth
craig wood

Gordon Matta-Clark:
rocking the foundation

The abbreviated bio might go something like this: Born Gordon Matta, 1943, the son of surrealist painter Roberto Matta Echaurren; grew up partly in Paris, mostly in New York; studied at the prestigious Cornell School of Architecture; supported most of his life by his estranged father. In 1971 he co-founded a 'health food' restaurant in SoHo called Food, where artists were sometimes guest-chefs.

He became the carver of whole buildings; he survived the suicide of his twin brother in 1976 and died less than two years later of pancreatic cancer en August 27, 1978. His was a brief but intense life; his career lasting barely ten years.

by Jeff Rian

In both content and look *Frieze* has always maintained a sophisticated cool style; simple, clear and uncluttered. It has grown and evolved but its core remains unchanged. 'It's quite interesting to look back at the pilot issue because all its contents are things that we've still got,' says Slotover. 'We've got older artists, younger artists, art stuff, a few non-art things,

artists' projects. So the contents haven't really changed that much. Design-wise the types changed, the grids have changed and now there's more colour.' *Frieze* was always aimed at and has always found an international audience. 'Our remit is international. Not many magazines are and it's one of our strengths I think that we try to bridge borders and try to let people know

what's going on here and vice versa,' Slotover clarifies. 'We publish only in English and sales are about one third UK, one third US and one third through the rest of the world – which includes Canada, Australia, New Zealand and Europe. We've just added quite a lot in the last year on the European side, with growing sales in countries like Scandinavia and Germany.'

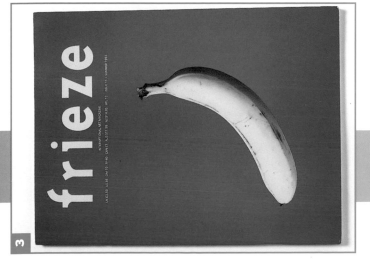

'SOMETIMES I THINK WE MIGHT LOSE A FEW THOUSAND SALES EACH ISSUE BECAUSE WE DON'T PUT THE CONTENTS ON THE COVER. MOST MAGAZINES DO, NOT BECAUSE IT LOOKS GOOD BUT BECAUSE IT'S A SALES TECHNIQUE. EDITORS OF OTHER MAGAZINES HAVE SAID TO ME "YOU'RE CRAZY, YOUR COVER'S YOUR BEST SALES TOOL!" BUT OUR READERS ARE SOPHISTICATED AND I HOPE – AND BELIEVE – THAT WE APPEAL TO PEOPLE WHO ARE WEARY OF THE USUAL SALES TECHNIQUE AND ARE ATTRACTED TO PUBLICATIONS AND PRODUCTS THAT ARE BOLD ENOUGH TO NOT USE THEM.'

'We don't have breakdowns of readership. Essentially *Frieze* is for people interested in contemporary art, but usual demographics break that down into such a broad range that those categories become meaningless. We know what's right for *Frieze* and essentially it's the stuff we are interested in, I think! The most interesting magazines are the ones where the editors are basically doing it for themselves and if they're lucky there are other people who share their sensibilities and if they're unlucky there aren't! Once you start thinking too much about your reader—I think you're in danger of your magazine and its contents becoming very bland. Our main competitors are obviously the art magazines; *Art Forum* in New York, *Flash Art* in Milan, *Parkett* in Zurich and *Art and Text*, which is from Australia. In the UK there is *Art Monthly* and *Contemporary Visual Arts*,' explains Slotover.

4 Issues 13 (left and far left) and 19 (below). Cover picture is Gavin Turk's 'Pop' (1993) photographed by Hugo Glendinning. 'We change the grid the whole time. We've always been much less reliant on traditional structures. I think the reason for that is the computer has made it much more flexible. You're not outputting lines of type anymore that you need to paste up and copy-fit into columns.'

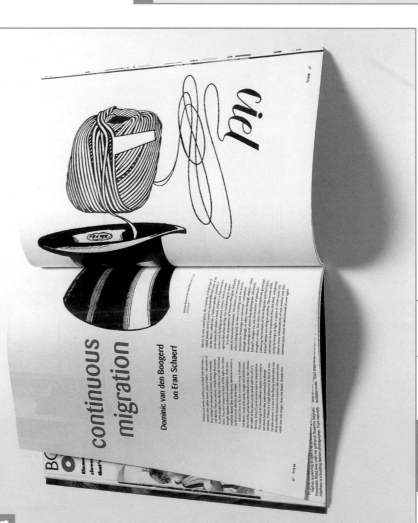

'THE MOST INTERESTING MAGAZINES ARE THE ONES WHERE THE EDITORS ARE BASICALLY DOING IT FOR THEMSELVES, AND IF THEY'RE LUCKY THERE ARE OTHER PEOPLE WHO SHARE THEIR SENSIBILITIES AND IF THEY'RE UNLUCKY THERE AREN'T! ONCE YOU START THINKING TOO MUCH ABOUT YOUR READER, I THINK YOU'RE IN DANGER OF YOUR MAGAZINE AND ITS CONTENTS BECOMING VERY BLAND.'

5 Issue 29. Cover picture is Jim Hodges' 'From Our Side' (1995). Titles are set in FF New Berlin, bold copy in FF Scala Sans and FF Quadraat.

Design and
working process

One of the most consistently striking aspects of *Frieze*'s design which differentiates it from its rivals and most other magazines, is its cover. With only the masthead and a carefully chosen picture it is a bold statement of style, identifying the nature of the contents without spelling them out. It grabs your attention and gives you no choice but to pick up an issue and browse if you want to know what's inside. The first few issues did list the subject matter using cover lines but very early on an editorial and design decision was made.

'Sometimes I think we might lose a few thousand sales each issue because we don't put the contents on the cover,' says Slotover, adding, 'Most magazines do it not because it looks good but because it's a sales technique. Editors of other magazines have said to me "you're crazy, your cover's your best sales tool!" But our readers are sophisticated and I hope – and believe – that we do more for people who are weary of the usual sales technique and are attracted to publications and products that are bold enough to not use them. *Frieze* is after all a specialist magazine.' If there is a loss in sales it's more than balanced by a gain in kudos. The minimal covers turn each issue into an object that can easily stand alongside the art inside, which is a perfect design solution given the subject material and the target audience. Obviously Slotover and Gidley were getting it right from the very beginning; issue three was nominated for a prestigious D&AD Silver Award for a 'Most Outstanding Cover'.

6 Issue 45. Cover picture is Steven Meisel's 'Cross-View' from Italian *Vogue* November 1998.

'We never have any problems with copy fitting – we can put 800 words over four pages or we can put it over one page, or 4,000 words over four pages or ten pages. Really that kind of decision is made at the very last minute when we have everything in, when we have the pictures and copy and can see how it looks and how it relates to other articles. We're extremely flexible in that way.'

The layout of the contents is entirely flexible from issue to issue. There is a strong continuity of look and style, but no fixed grids or typeface. The only consistent element is the masthead. 'We had a friend who did the logo in Illustrator. It hasn't changed at all since the beginning. It's adapted from Triplex, an Emigre font. *Frieze* has always been interested in design; we even ran a piece on Emigre in the pilot issue,' says Slotover. Originally *Frieze* used a different typeface for each issue. 'This was 1991 and '92,' Slotover elucidates: 'There were new fonts coming out the whole time and it was an exciting time in typeface design. So we didn't have to use the same fonts the whole time. And actually it was cheap – we used to get them sponsored, and we still do in exchange for a credit.' Looking back over early copies Slotover also notes: 'The magazine's editorial is now in sections, but it's not always been like that, we started off with no sections at all. Also there's a funny convention in art magazines, started I guess by *Art Forum* in the 1960s, that all the adverts go at the front and all the editorial goes together at the back. I think it was possibly because of the nature of art ads; they're useful as listing information so that people generally do read them front to back to see what's on. But there's also the question of impact – because these ads are mostly just type they would lose their impact next to features, unlike a lot of consumer ads in consumer magazines, which look as strong as editorial and therefore work better spread throughout the magazine.'

Techniques

Slotover has mixed feelings on new developments in printing and publishing: 'I'm looking forward to Adobe's InDesign – we're still using QuarkXPress version 3; the text tools and the justification are bad in Quark. We do our low-resolution scans here and the repro house does the high-resolution scanning. We're beginning to think about getting our own high-resolution scanners and probably do our own colour proofing here too, possibly outputting to PDF rather than film, and doing everything computer to plate so repro will disappear – thank god! There are always problems with scanning and colour correction, but bringing everything in-house should give us more creative freedom. I think it'll have a bad effect on deadlines though. At the moment we have to do our scans three days ahead, which means we have three days to fiddle about getting the layout exactly right. Once you have the ability to scan and proof yourself you don't have that three-day buffer, it just goes – I'm kind of nervous about that. Tom is not at all interested in the mechanics of it all and I think that's a benefit actually. He just wants the magazine to look as good as it can,' concludes Slotover.

7 Issue 46. Cover picture is Gerwald Rockenschaub's 'Inflatable Object' (1998). 'Although there is less experimentation with typefaces now, nothing is considered rigid and things are open to change with each issue. The nature of the articles dictate the accompanying pictures and *Frieze* never uses any illustrations and rarely commissions photographs.'

DETAILS
For subscriptions to *Frieze* tel: + 44 171 379 1533 or website: www. frieze.co.uk

HARDWARE/SOFTWARE
QuarkXPress 3.3, Photoshop 4.
Started on Mac SE Plus, now produced on Mac G3 266 with 196Mb ram.

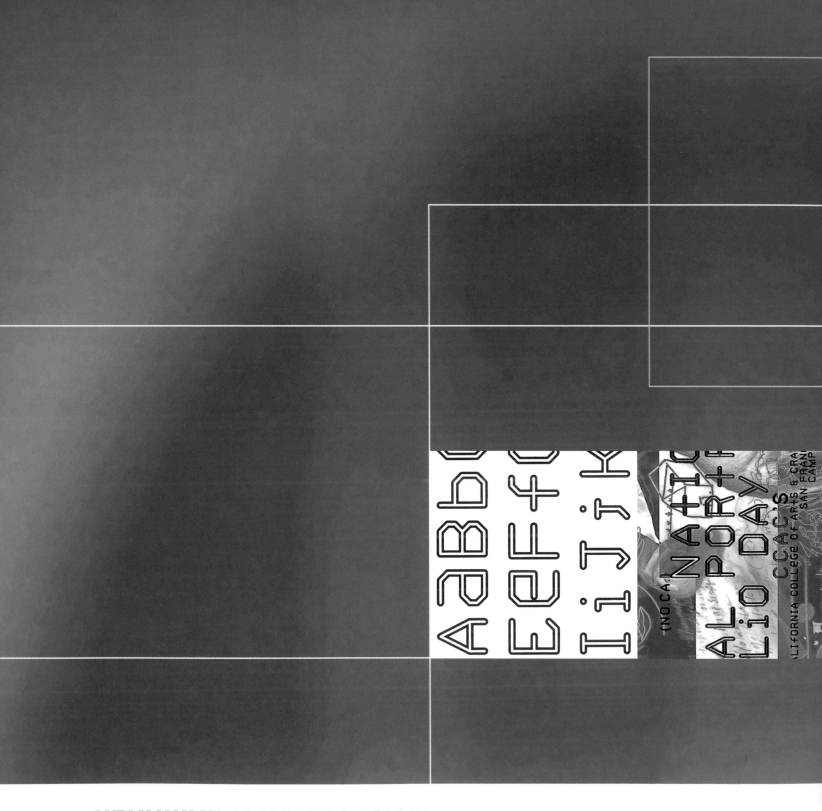

Biography

Northern California design group Aufuldish & Warinner, perhaps best known for partner Bob Aufuldish's roarShock dingbats typefaces, has clients ranging from record labels to petrochemical multinationals. Last year, Aufuldish & Warinner launched the fontBoy website, a digital typeface foundry that distributes digital typefaces which Aufuldish and others have designed. You might characterise the firm's work as baroque modernism.

Aufuldish teaches graphic design and typography at the California College of Arts and Crafts; and he designs and produces everything from posters to exhibitions, multimedia and books. He has also designed, photographed and produced two books about San Francisco. Partner Kathy Warinner has worked on packaging systems, websites, book and jacket design and illustrations for more than 20 book covers. Previously, at Landor Associates, she helped create corporate identities for clients such as the American Conservatory Theatre and Sun Microsystems.

grid of dots,
connected by lines.
different weights
of lines come of,
or all even.
different ways to connect
dots, more organic—
print out 4 me enough
w/ una. (re-drawn
by hand.)

'I DON'T HAVE A PROBLEM WITH CHANGES SO LONG AS THERE'S SOME REASONED OPINION BEHIND WHY THEY HAVE TO BE MADE – BUT IN THIS CASE I THINK THE POSTER WAS STRONGER VISUALLY WHEN THERE WERE MORE THINGS UP AT THE SAME SCALE...'

Background

In June 1998, the California College of Arts and Crafts asked Aufuldish & Warinner to design a poster for an event taking place in January 1999. 'There are a series of portfolio days for high schools, where kids come and show their work to someone and get a little bit of feedback. Every few years, the CCAC is the sponsor for Northern California and they're in charge of publicity,' says Aufuldish.

'The project they asked us to work on was a poster that would go to all the area high schools, to teachers and guidance counsellors, to help promote the event, as well as a postcard that the college would use to send to high school kids. They wanted it finished by October, and we started talking in June, so the lead time was pretty good,' he adds.

The firm had an existing relationship with CCAC. 'I teach at this college, and for the past

two or three summers I've worked out a deal with them where I'm on a retainer so I do everything for these certain few departments. I give them one price based on a list of projects, and this project was part of that,' explains Aufuldish.

The Project

Part of the project involved fitting in with CCAC's needs. 'It's been a long time since I was in a high-school art room, but the people at the college had some pretty specific ideas about how the poster had to function. The idea behind the poster and the postcard is that it's a page out of a sketchbook. There's a bunch of different media, a bunch of different drawing styles – it's like a big doodle.'

Cost, too, was an issue. 'The budget for both items was $4,000, for the typefaces and 14 variations altogether,' explains Aufuldish.

1. 'The client felt two of the initial three sketches presented, including this one, were too sophisticated, conceptually and visually, for the audience and the environment in which they would appear,' says Aufuldish.

2. The typeface used on the project, Punctual, emerged from a grid of dots, which Aufuldish connected to make the letterforms.

3. This alternate sketch by Kathy Warinner illustrates the idea behind the poster and the postcard, which is 'that it's a page out of a sketchbook. There's a bunch of different media, a bunch of different drawing styles – it's like a big doodle,' says Aufuldish.

4 CCAC was initially given three sketches, including this one (far left) on which the type had been approved. The big doodle drawn by Warinner was an integral part of all the initial presentations and was so liked by the college that with refining by Warinner it was kept on right through to the finished poster and postcard.

5 Some of Aufuldish's ideas were dictated by politics; for example the size of the letters CCAC had to be reduced, and the colleges' original setting of one continuous block of text whose line wrapped around had to be more clearly delineated, ending with one college on one line.

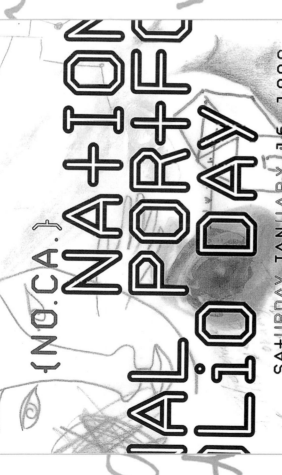

6 'The inline typeface, Punctual Four Inline, was very handy as a way to help pop the main title off the page,' says Aufuldish. 'The face also has a kind of goofy collegiate quality; there's all those Ivy League-looking typefaces that if you bought a sweatshirt from Harvard it would be set in that kind of type, and there are certain qualities about this type that allude to that, although this is much weirder – which is good, because it's for an art school,' he adds.

7 In the lighter versions of Punctual, the dots are large enough to be visible while the lines connecting them are very thin, but as Aufuldish developed and worked on the family the lines became thicker, until the line is as thick as the dot so that the dots disappear.

8 Other variations on the typeface included this one where the lowercase a is as tall as the uppercase A; 'a whole secondary set that functions in this way, which I call universal. The headline on the poster is a combination of characters. There's no one version of the font where if you type what you see you would get what is there – I went through and substituted characters from the universal and from the regular inline typefaces, 14 variations altogether,' explains Aufuldish.

> 'THERE'S SOMETHING INTERESTING ABOUT A VERY STRAIGHTFORWARD STRUCTURE, STRAIGHTFORWARD TYPOGRAPHY, PRESSED UP AGAINST SOME ODDER TYPOGRAPHY. OFTEN I SEE THINGS WHERE EVERYTHING ABOUT THE TYPOGRAPHY IS GOOFY IN SOME WAY, AND IT'S NOT REALLY CLEAR WHETHER OR NOT THE DESIGNER IS IN CONTROL OF THAT. DID THEY JUST LUCK OUT AND IT'S GREAT, OR DOES THIS THING REALLY FUNCTION IN THE WAY THEY INTENDED?'

7

AaBbCcDd
EeFfGgHh
IiJjKkLl
MmNnOo
PpQqRrSs
TtUuVvWw
XxYyZzI2
34567890

6

AaBbCcDd
EeFfGgHh
IiJjKkLl
MmNnOo
PpQqRrSs
TtUuVvWw
XxYyZzI2
34567890

AaBbCcDd
EeFfGgHh
IiJjKkLl
MmNnOo
PpQqRrSs
TtUuVvWw
XxYyZzI2
34567890

AaBbCcDd
EeFfGgHh
IiJjKkLl
MmNnOo
PpQqRrSs
TtUuVvWw
XxYyZzI2
34567890

AaBbCcDd
EeFfGgHh
IiJjKkLl
MmNnOo
PpQqRrSs
TtUuVvWw
XxYyZzI2
34567890

AaBbCcDd
EeFfGgHh
IiJjKkLl
MmNnOo
PpQqRrSs
TtUuVvWw
XxYyZzI2
34567890

8

AaBbCcDd
EeFfGgHh
IiJjKkLl
MmNnOo
PpQqRrSs
TtUuVvWw
XxYyZzI2
34567890·

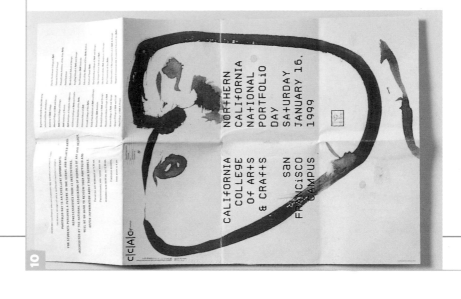

9 Aufuldish meticulously churns out print-outs that may differ minutely: 'Each one is like looking at another subtle little thing I'm trying to evaluate within everything else,' he says.

10 Because the budget for both poster and postcard was just $4,000, Aufuldish & Warinner designed the poster to fold down so it could self-mail, with the address going in the white space under the words 'CCAS Campus'.

Development

'Kathy did the sketch first,' says Aufuldish, which he scanned in and designed 'right on top of it.' He took CCAC three sketches: 'At the first meeting they chose a direction very similar to the final... the one with the big doodle. In the first couple of initial presentations I used that big sketch until the client at one point said, "Hey, are you guys going to redo this drawing?"'

'I said, "Well, if you like it, we'll just use it." That conversation led them to analyse the sketch a little more carefully and then they started getting a little more picky, so at that point Kathy redrew it larger and tighter. Then I did another presentation with a poster based on that drawing,' says Aufuldish.

Adjusting the font sizes of the various textual elements on the poster's front was Aufuldish's biggest headache. 'At first I thought it was just going to be National Portfolio Day, the date, and the college. By the time we were done it was all that plus the name of every college that was going to appear, a logo for the sponsoring organisation – all of this MUCK. So we made it all blue space.'

Politics dictated some of the client's decisions. 'We had to make the hierarchy of information work in a way that the client was comfortable with. At first I had the name of the college at the same size as National Portfolio Day, because it was my understanding that this was part of the sell for local high-school kids. The client realised it made the college too important – partly because the budget for the poster came from a fee that all the colleges pay, so they didn't want the other colleges to feel they were paying to promote CCAC.' Aufuldish dutifully made the name of the college smaller.

Also in this version, he says, 'There were 32 colleges, so what I did in a typical crabby designer way was to put them in a solid block of text. I made that block a funny shape; you might be reading along in that block and halfway through the name of the school the line ends and it picks up in the next line – and boy, that didn't go over very well. In the final, you'll see each school is on a separate line.'

PUNCTUAL EMERGED FROM '...JUST THIS GOOFY LITTLE IDEA THAT I HAD ABOUT CONNECTING DOTS. I MADE THIS GRID OF DOTS AND I JUST STARTED PLAYING AROUND WITH IT, CONNECTING THOSE DOTS TO MAKE THE LETTER FORMS. I STARTED LOOKING AT WHAT KIND OF RANGE OF POSSIBILITIES THERE WERE WITHIN THIS.'

11

12

11

Technique

Aufuldish's working methods vary. His first work on Punctual consists of 'a sketch in my sketchbook where I made a bunch of dots and connected them together very roughly, then wrote a little note that explained what I was thinking. Then from time to time I would just go through and see if there was something really compelling, because drawing type takes forever, so whatever idea there is behind the type has to be compelling enough to blow half a year on.'

11
'What I really like about this poster is that the image is this free-form, kind of floaty thing, and then the type on top of it appears to be free-form and floating as well, but it's really not – everything in there lines up with something else,' says Aufuldish. 'I'm very, very fond of internally structuring typography. For example, with the poster, there might be a little something way, way up at the top that appears to be floating, but then when you start analysing the way the poster's structured, you realise it's really lining up with some other little element, and then that creates some kind of visual line that some other elements play off of.'

12
'Only way, way towards the end of the process did we reverse the drawing,' says Aufuldish. 'It was literally the last presentation I did where it was a blue drawing on white, and I had done both of them and I just said, "today we've got to pick, which one do you like?" and they said, "We like the blue one," and I said, "okay, it's the blue one!"'

13
CCAC wanted a postcard that it could use to send to high school children. This sketch for the postcard was based on the already approved poster type.

Then, he says, 'It's like an epiphany. If you saw the first sketch I did for new clear era, (a font he designed for his elder daughter, Emily) and then you saw the typeface, you would understand where it came from but you would not say, "oh, the final typeface looks like the sketch". Some of the structural ideas are there, some of the ideas about how to decorate the structure of the letters, but literally the way they are drawn is not present in the final,' he explains.

'Depending on where you are in the process, it can be very methodical. I can show you variation after variation after variation where it would be pretty hard for you to know what I had done – actually, a year later it'd be hard for me to tell you, but at the time each print-out is like looking at another subtle little thing I'm trying to evaluate within everything else. You just beat on this stuff until it works.'

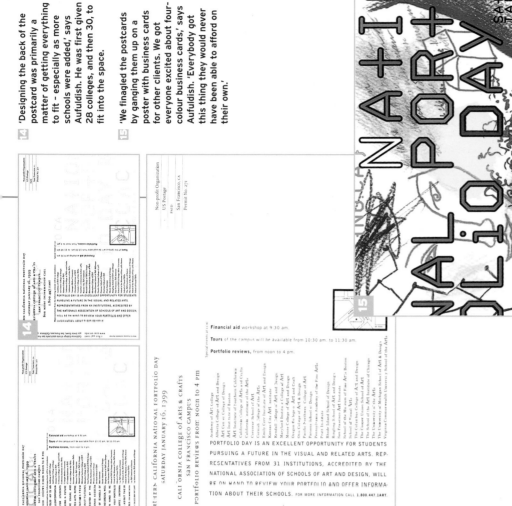

14 'Designing the back of the postcard was primarily a matter of getting everything to fit – especially as more schools were added,' says Aufuldish. He was first given 28 colleges, and then 30, to fit into the space.

15 'We finagled the postcards by ganging them up on a poster with business cards for other clients. We got everyone excited about four-colour business cards,' says Aufuldish. 'Everybody got this thing they would never have been able to afford on their own.'

DETAILS
Aufuldish & Warinner
183 The Alameda
San Anselmo, CA 94960, USA
tel: +1 415 721 7921 (Bob)
tel: +1 415 721 7920 (Kathy)
fax: +1 415 721 7965
email: info@fontboy.com
URL: http://www.fontboy.com/

CLIENTS
Warner Brothers Records, Apple Computer, the Chevron Corporation. The Nature Company, Emigre Graphics, Harper Collins and Speak magazine.

CREDITS
Design and project management: Bob Aufuldish
Illustration: Kathy Warinner

HARDWARE/SOFTWARE
Microtech Scanmaker 2 scanner, PowerMac 8500/180 with 64K RAM, Illustrator 6 (the mechanicals were done in this).

Background

While web design is now becoming a firmly established design discipline, and early problems – such as use of fonts not on the users' computers, slow download time for large graphics etc. – have been tackled and overcome by a marriage of technology and a design sensibility around working with the medium, there are still problems that face practitioners in this area. For example, how do you go about creating a website in not just three languages, but three entirely different scripts? This was the problem facing Lemon, a four-year-old Hong Kong-based interactive design agency founded by CEO and creative director David Mok, when the company was invited to pitch for a Nike website targeting the Pacific Rim. Fortunately, Lemon's main area of expertise is in developing advanced websites, a question of 'combining design perfection and intelligent technology', says Yvette Yanne, production manager of the company which also produces CD-ROMs, touch-screen kiosks, videos and print work.

Yanne describes the culture of the company as 'very open, relaxed and non-hierarchical, everyone has shares in the company. We currently have 12 members of staff, all relatively young, in our twenties and thirties, and from very diverse backgrounds such as graphic design, multimedia, film and TV, publishing, computing, networking, banking and architecture.' Although the company is based in Hong Kong, its staff is drawn from countries including Hong Kong, the UK, the US and France. Clients include AT&TmySite, Turner Asia Pacific Inc., British Airways, Shanghai Tang, Kerry Properties, South China Morning Post and Schindler.

'IT'S A FACT THAT IF YOU USE CHINESE SCRIPT AS PART OF THE OVERALL DESIGN, IT INSTANTLY MAKES THAT DESIGN LOOK AND FEEL CHINESE, SO WE TRIED TO MAKE THE TYPOGRAPHY INTEGRAL TO THE OVERALL DESIGNS.'

歡迎

enter

flash version

The brief

While the worldwide Nike site, Nike.com, was being accessed globally, the company was aware that the site was designed to speak to one homogeneous audience – Americans. Outside the US, it had little or no relevance, and was failing to serve local markets. To that end, Nike decided it needed an Asia-Pacific site in order to address the region. It developed the idea of splitting the region into three markets; Japan, Greater China and Australia. The audience had been identified as, primarily, 12-24 year old males and, secondarily, 15-35 years old males and females. Nike approached three interactive agencies in Hong Kong to see who could best demonstrate a communications vehicle speaking to Asia-Pacific's fragmented audience. The brief was pretty loose, and gave us a high degree of creativity in all areas,' says Roselyn Cheung, managing director of the company.

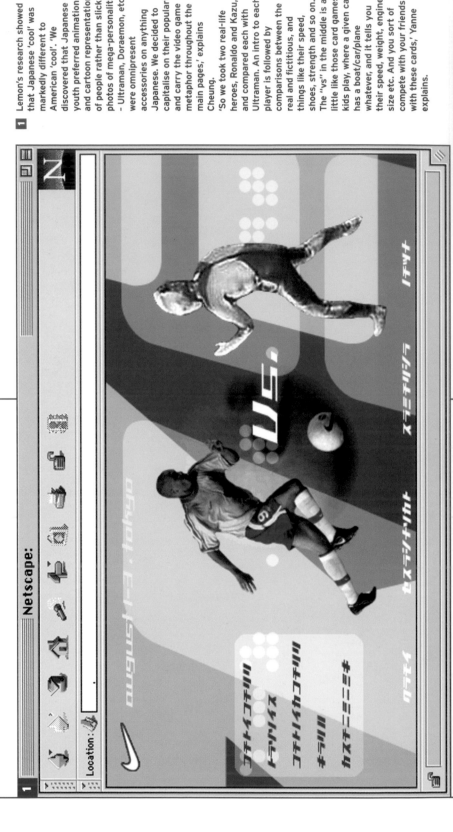

Lemon's research showed that Japanese 'cool' was markedly different to American 'cool'. 'We discovered that Japanese youth preferred animations and cartoon representations of people rather than slick photos of mega-personalities – Ultraman, Doraemon, etc. were omnipresent accessories on anything Japanese. We decided to capitalise on their popularity and carry the video game metaphor throughout the main pages,' explains Cheung.

'So we took two real-life heroes, Ronaldo and Kazu, and compared each with Ultraman. An intro to each player is followed by comparisons between the real and fictitious, and things like their speed, shoes, strength and so on. The "vs" in the middle is a little like those card games kids play, where a given card has a boat/car/plane whatever, and it tells you their speed, weight, engine size etc. And you sort of compete with your friends with these cards,' Yanne explains.

Nike's requests were:

1 A home page and links to the core nike.com site.
2 A mock football training clinic led by Ronaldo of Brazil and Kazu of Japan.
3 An explanation of Lemon's servicing plan and its ability to work with an external lead creative agency.

Additionally, 'Nike invited us to surprise them with our creative juices,' says Cheung.

The requirements for the site were:

1 Quick downloads.
2 Product demonstrations.
3 The ability to collect user information into a database.
4 Sensitivity to censorship policies.

The paid pitch from Lemon took the form of a multimedia presentation which included designs for the three websites, a flowchart showing the structure of the website and mood videos for each site. It was backed up by a Powerpoint presentation showing facts and figures of the different markets.

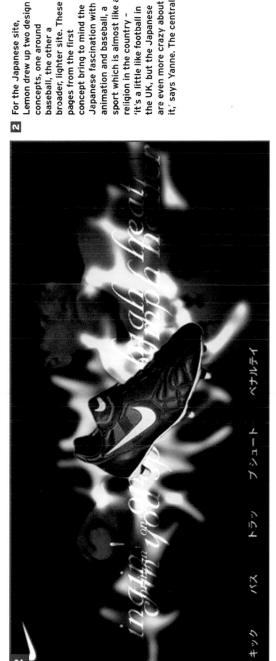

For the Japanese site, Lemon drew up two design concepts, one around baseball, the other a broader, lighter site. These pages from the first concept bring to mind the Japanese fascination with animation and baseball, a sport which is almost like a religion in the country – 'it's a little like football in the UK, but the Japanese are even more crazy about it,' says Yanne. The central image of the baseball player and a background of simple colours are designed to 'suggest an explosion and an object or player coming out of the page, signifying their importance. The dual language is not a problem in terms of design, because actually the Japanese (and Chinese) script works really well with English on a page. But here the Japanese text is dummy text,' she adds.

'THE NAVIGATION FOR ANY WEBSITE IS MORE THAN THE LOOK OF IT, IT'S MUCH MORE TO DO WITH FUNCTIONALITY AND USER-FRIENDLINESS. IT MUST BE CLEAR AND CONCISE ENOUGH FOR USERS TO UNDERSTAND AND BE ABLE TO ENCOURAGE A TRAFFIC FLOW THROUGH THE SITE. THEN IT BECOMES PART OF THE INTERFACE DESIGN.'

3

Research and development

Initial brain-storming sessions after digestion of the brief led to individual sites being designed for each of the local markets, i.e. one site for Japan, one site for Pan-China and one for Australia. 'Since the nature of the markets was so different this seemed the best way of communicating with each one, as individual sites would allow us to hone in on the language, cultural nuances and sporting attitudes of the local audience,' explains Cheung. The company split into teams, each of which included an art director, programmer and project manager. Each team was responsible for research into each market and coming up with a few concepts/approach. 'It was a very intense and energetic time, as we only had two weeks to work on the pitch, during which all the teams met up again and discussed all the ideas and their various aspects,' says Cheung. 'Everyone kept an eye out for anything related to sports in their market. Project managers specifically researched the demographics on computer usage, Internet knowledge and stats on the sporting habits of each market,' she adds. The majority of the research was conducted online, supplemented by materials found in local libraries and Lemon affiliates in Japan and Australia. 'We concentrated our research into the sports related area, but also the overlap between sports fans and Internet users. We also looked at fashion, lifestyle, media and trends, and at Nike's competitors' sites, i.e., Adidas, Reebok, Puma, Fila, etc. We were looking for other demonstrations of interactivity, use of language, graphic style and scripts, and star power. And finally we also interviewed people from these markets – talking to people gave us a lot of information and ideas,' explains Cheung.

Working process and techniques

As Nike had hinted that Japan was the most important market, Lemon focused its energies on getting that site right, before working on its Chinese and Australian counterparts. 'To fully understand the different style and techniques, we looked at a lot of different media – books, magazines, print ads, websites, TV, video etc. –

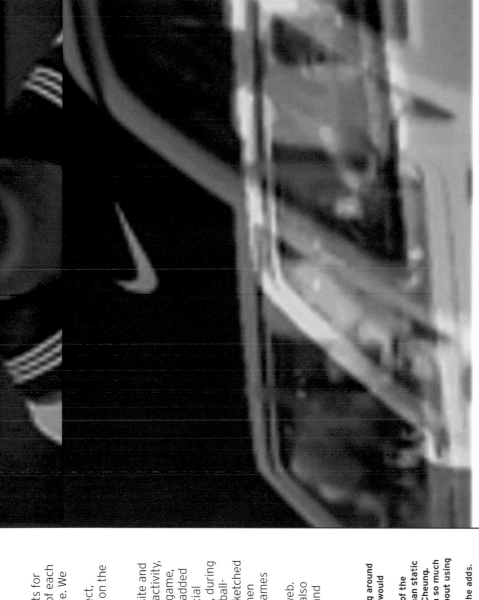

when dealing with the scripts and layouts for each region,' says Cheung. 'The design of each site came after the concept and storyline. We tried to make it clear that each site is distinctive and focused in a certain aspect, each site had a theme. Then we worked on the design,' she adds.

In a bid to promote repeat visits to the site and attract users who were looking for interactivity, Lemon decided each site was to have a game, with the idea that new games would be added periodically, and in particular when special events or seasons started – for example, during the World Cup the games would be football-based. The concept of each game was sketched out in storyboards, and graphics were then done in Photoshop and Freehand. The games were put together in Director, and later exported as Shockwave for use on the web. Graphics for the sites themselves were also created mainly using Photoshop, Freehand and Illustrator.

3 Lemon devised these video mood-boards as an alternative to the more traditional two-dimensional mood-boards used in design and advertising pitches. 'We believed that seeing real live people wearing Nike clothes, doing sports, shopping around town and so on would give a better representation of the Nike attitude than static pictures,' says Cheung. 'Nike liked them so much they thought about using them as TV commercials!' she adds.

'WEBSITES ARE NOT ELECTRONIC CATALOGUES. THEY'RE LIVING ORGANISMS THAT SHOULD STIMULATE AND SUSTAIN THE INTEREST OF YOUR VISITORS SO THAT THEY'LL KEEP COMING BACK. THEY'RE DEVELOPED ON THE BASIS OF AN EVOLUTIONARY PROCESS, CREATED THROUGH AN ONGOING PROACTIVE PARTNERSHIP.'

'CHINESE CONSUMERS OF NIKE PRODUCTS LIVE IN URBAN AREAS, WITH HIGH DISPOSABLE INCOMES AND LEISURE TIME. WE THOUGHT THEY MIGHT RELATE TO THE GRAFFITI-STYLE TYPEFACE. THIS WAS ORIGINAL "CALLIGRAPHY", WRITTEN WITH THE TRADITIONAL *MAO BI*. WE THOUGHT THIS METHOD WOULD IMMEDIATELY CONVEY A CONNECTION WITH CHINESE SPEAKERS, AS WELL AS A PSEUDO-REBELLIOUS ATTITUDE.'

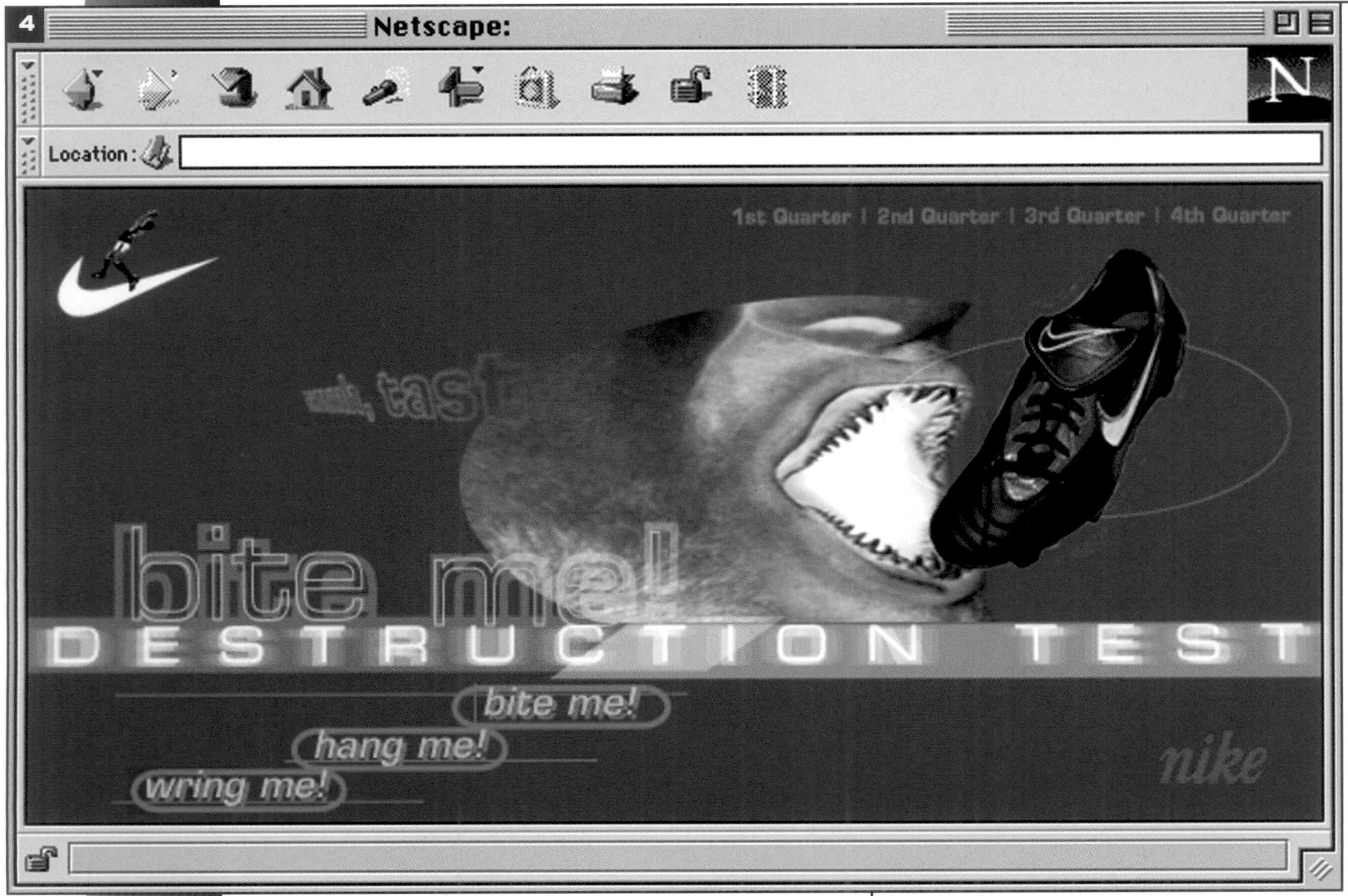

The three sites: Japan

Lemon created two design concepts for this site, one of which focused on the country's most popular sport, baseball, the other a lighter and more humorous site which took Japanese footballer and national hero Kazu and Brazilian striker Ronaldo and compared them to Ultraman, a popular superhero character in Japan. Lemon's research had shown that the brand Nike meant 'trend-setting' and 'fashionable' to the Japanese, rather than 'sports'. They also found that the Japanese were very influenced by popular culture such as video games, pop idols and animation, so decided to make their designs more about lifestyle; 'more funky and fun, rather than focused on sports in a serious manner,' says Yanne. The researchers also found that the Japanese like collecting things, whether it be stamps, comics or Nike trainers, and take the hobby very seriously – 'so we devised a section called "Nike Time Machine", sort of an online Nike museum which featured every single product Nike has ever released in Japan, with extensive photographs and information about each product,' explains Yanne.

Netscape:
Location:

nike

bite me!
DESTRUCTION TEST

1st Quarter | 2nd Quarter | 3rd Quarter | 4th Quarter

taste me!

bite me!
hang me!
wring me!

map

injury

Kicking
Marking
Hand Pass
Rules

2,467 wrecked knees
some zillions of sprained ankles

4 **Australia**
The target market in Australia was found to be real sports players playing a variety of sports. The emphasis on football in the site's pages came from the research Lemon conducted into the playing of those sports in Australia: 'Footie seemed to be one of the dominant sports played, and from games and interviews we watched, we learned that the people who make a career out of it do so at great physical expense. And in print, interview after interview listed the number of ways you could injure yourself playing the game,' says Cheung. 'We decided to use a lot of Australian lingo and humour, but were careful not to make fun of any sports. This site is more product-driven, more technical than the other two regions,' says Cheung.

4 Lemon developed the "Aussie Rules" or Footie section of the Australian site because it is an indigenous sport to the area. The slightly tongue-in-cheek machismo feel to the site was something Lemon felt was appropriate because 'we felt Australians had a self-deprecating humour and lingo that we could incorporate into the site,' says Cheung.

Netscape:

Location:

nike

5 This page on the China site shows the football penalty shoot-out game. The four round colour buttons read China, Hong Kong, Taiwan and Singapore, the four countries the Pan-China site caters for. Users are invited to click left or right of the football diagram on the right, in order to vote which way the goalkeeper will dive. 'The idea was that the game would be updated weekly, and each week a different region would be taking the penalties, with the others in goal,' says Yanne. A link underneath the football diagram shows last week's results and also links to a page with a quicktime video/ animation of the shoot-out. The chart at bottom left shows the statistics for the shoot-out.

6 Because of the nature of Chinese type and the local graphic design style, Lemon was able to play with various structures and layouts, so this basketball page looks and feels very different to the rest of the site. 'We tried to have a slightly different feel for each section of the site, in order to make it more dynamic and give it a feel of energy throughout,' says Yanne.

China

This site was actually going to cover greater China, so would include countries such as Hong Kong, Taiwan and Singapore – in all, an audience of some 15 billion Chinese. Lemon's research unsurprisingly showed that the culture and markets in these countries were actually quite different and that the only common currency was the language – 'and even that has different dialects, writing and local slang,' says Yanne. But as each individual market was not really developed enough or large enough to warrant its own site, Lemon decided the way forward lay with an idea of 'global Chinese'. 'We played with a Chinese saying, loosely translated as ''Chinese people don't kill Chinese people'', which basically means you don't harm your own people,' says Yanne. This theme of solidarity was graphically realised on the site with a game featuring a football penalty shoot-out, in which Chinese from different regions vote on which way the goalkeeper is going to dive. 'It stresses the regionality of the site and the togetherness of its people using a fair degree of humour,' says Yanne.

Yanne believes the paid pitch for Nike was 'by far our best work'. The interface and navigation designs, artwork, games, flowcharts and mood videos for each region proved to be one of the company's most extensive pitches, and the involvement of the three different languages made it a rare and complex piece of web design. Sadly, it was never fully developed and published because, in the face of a worsening Asian economic crisis, Nike pulled out of Hong Kong after the pitches had been presented and moved the project to Japan.

'Because Chinese script are traditionally read vertically, we played with the notion of reading top to bottom, left to right. It gave us much more freedom to express ourselves and allowed more creativity in layout design. On the Chinese home page, the images change as you roll over the various sections, much like a display board at a train terminal. Arranging the buttons as we did allowed interactivity with the graphics,' says Cheung. The headlines and graffiti-style faces were done as graphics.

7 'This is the Nike League, a HK youth basketball championship we invented in order to show Nike how it could sponsor such leagues and events. The white mountain-range-type signifies a Chinese saying, which loosely translates as "there's always a mountain higher than yours", meaning there's always someone better, so don't be too big-headed or competitive,' explains Yanne. 'The text gives information about the league, and if it were a real league the page and links would include live video, sound, photos, scoreboards and so on.'

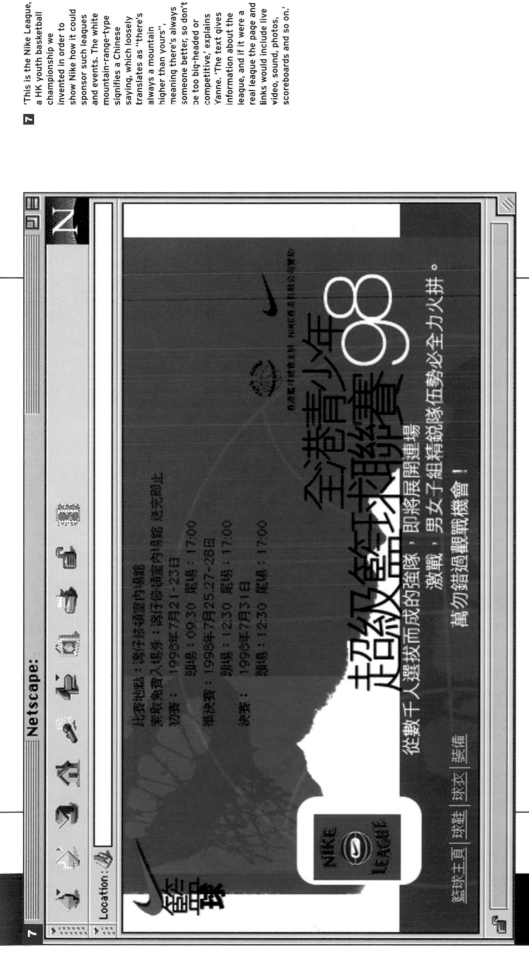

HARDWARE/SOFTWARE
Macs, PCs, Media 100, Sony DV.
Freehand, Photoshop, Director, Illustrator, Premiere,
Sound Edit.

DETAILS
Lemon (HK) Ltd.
12th floor, Tin On Sing Commercial Building
41-43 Graham Street, Central
Hong Kong
tel: + 852 2537 2313
fax: + 852 2537 9744
e-mail: lemon@lemon.com.hk
website: http://www.lemon.com.hk

STABLE ENOUGH TO WITHST

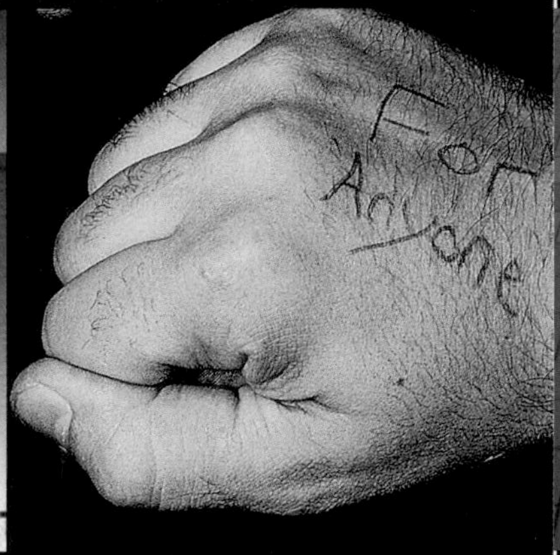

For Anyone

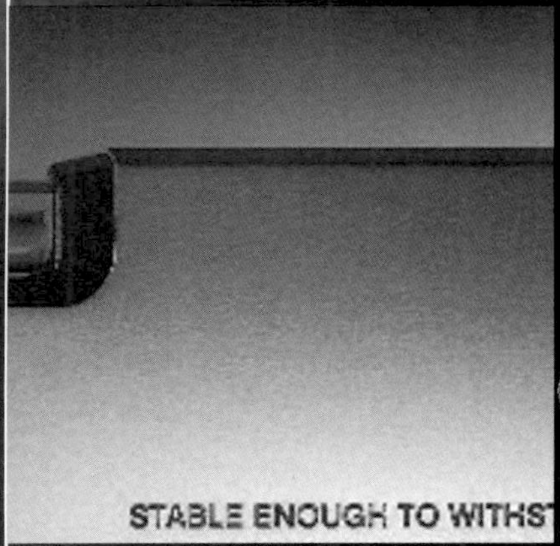

Biography

Michael Johnson, head of London design consultancy Johnson Banks, is complaining about web designers. He has been playing around with an animation package and after some experimenting has found it remarkably easy to use, so he's feeling a bit miffed with those multimedia designers who like to make a song and dance of their art. Is he planning to take up web design then? 'No', he smiles, refusing to be drawn further on the discipline. Perhaps when you are as accomplished a graphic designer as Johnson, you don't need to diversify to keep the creative juices flowing. And there is no doubting that he is one of Europe's finest graphic designers, as evidenced by regular awards and commendations from the likes of D&AD, The Art Directors' Club of New York,

Design Week and the BBC Design Awards. Johnson Banks will happily undertake every aspect of a design job, including writing and even, for a William Morris exhibition held at London's Victoria & Albert Museum in 1996, type design. Based on Morris's own late experiments with calligraphy, the face designed by the company is what Johnson calls 'modern, not a medieval imitation' and 'something Morris would hopefully approve of.'

With a joint degree in design and marketing you would expect Johnson's work to show equal strength in both design and copywriting, and on many of his seven-year-old company's past projects that has been the case; for the BBC Design Awards, the company entered a series of public information posters it had done for Southeast Railways' stations which showed things like a man's toupee being swept off its owner's head with the copyline 'watch out for air turbulence'. It originally read 'hair turbulence' but the pun was deemed too punsome. For the past six years, Johnson has been designing and writing the copy for Skye Papers' promotional literature, a job which has incorporated the design of brochures, calendars and associated literature for what Johnson calls 'a target audience which is tricky and very difficult to impress', namely graphic designers who might be persuaded to specify Skye papers.

'TYPE IS THE ILLUSTRATION OF THE '90s... IN THE '80s, ILLUSTRATION WAS EVERYWHERE, THEN IT JUST SEEMED TO DIE OUT AND TYPE TOOK ITS PLACE - ON FILMS, POSTERS, TV STINGS, EVERYWHERE. I THINK IT'S A TRICKLE-DOWN EFFECT FROM THINGS LIKE GERT DUNBAR TEACHING AT THE RCA AND GRAHAM WOODS AND TOMATO'S WORK. BUT I THINK IT'S ON THE WAY OUT. I DON'T THINK THE SKYE BROCHURE IS AN EXAMPLE OF WHAT WILL REPLACE IT, BUT IT IS A REACTION AGAINST IT.'

Background and Brief

Johnson's association with Skye began in 1991 with the Natural White Brochure. The 'grand theme' behind this early series of work was 'Treasure of the World', which ran for two years. Associated merchandising such as calendars strengthened the brand and carried the theme throughout the year. 'I tried to deal with the idea of treasures in an interesting way, so rather than just physical, worldly treasures, we shot things like natural treasures and even emotional ones – love is a treasure, for example, as is freedom, so we would try and represent those ideals graphically through iconography such as the African continent with South Africa highlighted on it,' explains Johnson.

The 'Treasures' series was followed by a 'How' series of pamphlets, which ran for seven issues and was created 'as an antidote to the masses

of useless literature put out by the hundreds of paper mills and manufacturers,' says Johnson. 'They spend a lot of money on literature which is sent out to an incredibly knowledgeable and critical audience, and a lot of the time, once it's been assessed as a piece of design it's binned or filed away. And often the promotional material doesn't actually influence the buyer at all. I call it the soap powder syndrome: most people stick with one soap powder, regardless of marketing pushes from brand competitors. They know it, they're comfortable with it, they don't think about it,' he adds. What the 'How' series offered was useful information on printing effects, print saturation, using metallics and so on. It was so successful an idea that Johnson says designers were phoning Skye asking for more copies, and they actually ran out of some of the series.

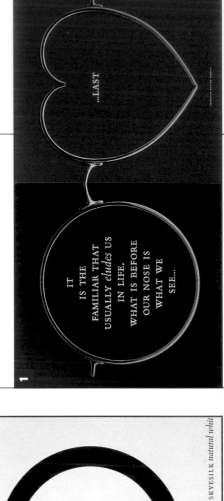

1 Michael Johnson's relationship with Skye began in the early '90s with these 'grand theme' brochures which dealt with treasures of the world. In the following year, the theme was broadened to bigger subjects, such as treasures like freedom and love.

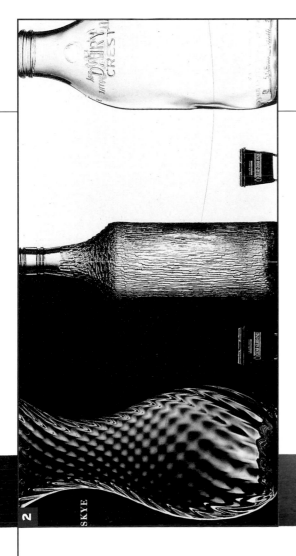

2 Related work for the client: part of a campaign for a recycled addition, a page from a calendar and an exhibition for Skye's advisory service, with a specially made paper alphabet.

3 The most recent campaign dealt with 'How' to achieve certain printing effects. It ran for seven issues before Johnson decided to 'pare things back to basics'.

'BECAUSE THE TARGET AUDIENCE IS SO TRICKY AND SO DIFFICULT TO IMPRESS, INCORPORATING THE TYPOGRAPHY INTO EVERY IMAGE IS MUCH MORE DIFFICULT AND IN A WEIRD KIND OF WAY WINS THEIR RESPECT. IT WAS ALSO A WAY TO KEEP US ON OUR TOES – PART OF A PROJECT LIKE THIS IS THINKING OF WAYS TO KEEP YOURSELF ALIVE, MENTALLY, WHEN YOU ARE DEALING WITH SIMILAR MESSAGES YEAR AFTER YEAR.'

7

7

‡TABLE ENOUGH TO WITHSTAND ALL PRINT PROCESSES

Development and working process

While it was incredibly successful, after two years of the 'How' series, Johnson says he felt it was time to go back to zero and design something very simple, and very different. Eschewing the 'grand themes' of the past six years' work on the Skye range, he decided to concentrate on promoting the qualities of Skye's range in a very simple but eye-catching way. 'From the initial concept, we needed a very straightforward idea. As the brochure was meant as a definite back-to-basics approach, we started with the simplest sentences we could write that described the paper and the range. But those sentences look pretty dull written down, so we wanted to bring them to life, and by exploring vernacular typography we thought it would be a good way to bring the message home,' says Johnson. 'Sure, we could have just taken a nice photo of a lot of different sized shoes and put a bit of type underneath, but that would have been dull,' he adds.

4

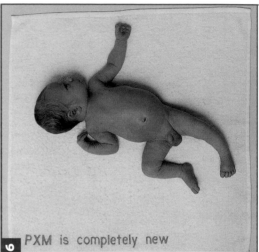

6 PXM is completely new

5 SKYE

4 'Sarah (Fullerton) and the photographer Mark Guthrie both wrote the words "...and completely unique" on the albino man's chest in lipstick, but on reflection we preferred the photographer's handwriting! Maybe they make good typographers!'

5 The simplicity of the brochure's cover reflects the back-to-basics feel of the project.

6 The new-born baby ('actually an eight-day-old baby, very hard to find and luckily a friend's!' says Johnson) laying on the towel embroidered with 'PMX is completely new', (promoting the new PMX range) was originally a full-body shot, but a James McNaughton board director said he didn't want the brochure to look like a Benetton ad, so we had to crop the photo to just above the genitalia, which is a shame because this original picture's actually much nicer!' says Johnson.

7 In order to create realistic shots, Johnson Banks commissioned model-makers to come up with the spirit level, loaf, glass slides and cheque book. 'They were thankfully relatively easy to shoot, though because glass is difficult to shoot well, I think the photographer Mark Grimwade did a very good job with the slides,' says Johnson.

8 This shot by photographer Gary Salter was achieved using a step ladder, a Land Rover and Gary's typography skills.

9 After Michael and co-designer on the project Sarah Fullerton came up with the idea of images incorporating key words around the properties of the Skye range, they had to simply refine and realise those ideas. Their initial idea for a row of shoes to illustrate the size of the range used men's shoes, which were then replaced with women's stilettos; but the idea didn't change.

'IT'S A NICE WAY TO LOOK AT THE WORLD WHEN YOU THINK OF EVERY SIGN OR HANDWRITTEN NOTE OR MAGNETIC FRIDGE MAGNET BEING YOUR NEXT PIECE OF TYPE, RATHER THAN THE LATEST £40 FONT RELEASE WHICH ONCE YOU'VE CHOSEN IT WILL IMMEDIATELY TIME LOCK YOUR WORK, WHETHER THAT FONT BE META OR TEMPLATE GOTHIC OR WHATEVER.'

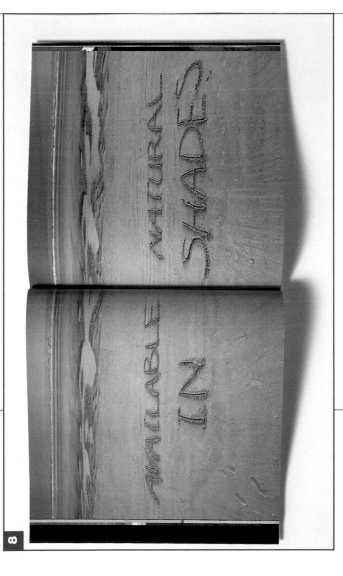

8

Once the ideas for each spread – covering smoothness, coatings, range, print stability, tints, the new PMX paper, testing, custom ordering, bulk and price – had been formulated, it became a straightforward process of sourcing and producing the images: finding the model-makers, photographers and locations.
'Each of the original shots posed its own problems, from the physical to the aesthetic, but it was only the swimming pool that

required major retouching and computer intervention. It was quite complex – complex enough for us to subcontract out the re-touching job to Steve Warner anyway! The shoes posed a different problem, as they were a nightmare to shoot. We started with an overhead rostrumed camera that after hours and hours of unsuccessful shooting attempts ended up at floor level to really capture that sense of perspective as the sizes get smaller, which was the point of it!

'The spirit level, loaf, glass slides and cheque book were made by model-makers and thankfully they were relatively easy to shoot, though because glass is difficult to shoot well I think the photographer Mark Grimwade did a very good job with the slides. On the beach shot, photographer Gary Salter, who chose the location, turned typographer when he wrote out the words "Available in natural shades" in the sand – you can see his footprints and we debated whether to keep those or not. We decided it was more natural to keep them,' says Johnson. From initial concept through to finished brochure, the design changed very little, as evidenced by the fact that the initial mock-up brochure produced by Johnson Banks is remarkably similar to the finished product.

9

It would seem Johnson Banks has once again got its finger on the pulse of graphic design, as the Skye brochure this year made it into the 'notoriously difficult to get into' typography section of D&AD. I asked Michael Johnson why a piece of design that has so little type in it would be honoured in this category: 'Perhaps it's part of an overall boredom with all that showy, layered stuff that's around which has started to look anything but cutting edge, more like blunt edge. Also, I think you just have to work that bit harder to get things read at the moment. I've personally been quite taken with the ugly/vernacular/found typography approach for some time now, just because I think we all (myself included) got pretty good at knocking out great looking type. I'm more interested now in wrong-looking type because that wrongness has become more appealing.'

So while on the surface it may seem that the computer played little part in the design of the Skye brochure, it's apparent that this approach is a distinct reaction to the ubiquitousness of computer-generated type. Is it the start of something big? 'Whether this approach will kick off a huge binge on found type, who knows. If it does, we will hopefully have moved on to something else by then. All we've done is broadened our approach to "typography" as far as we possibly can to incorporate anything and everything that we see around us,' answers Johnson.

10 The designers simply employed Quark and Photoshop to amalgamate four shots into the one spread which appears in the brochure.

11 From the outset, Johnson Banks knew that actually writing words in the bottom of a pool was unfeasible, and luckily found this pool – just around the corner from the studio – whose tile patterns formed a grid with which they could create the necessary type using Photoshop. Johnson says capturing the sense of shadows, light and shading as they move across the letters in the pool was difficult enough to warrant subcontracting the work to Steve Warner, who manipulated the image using Photoshop and Live Picture.

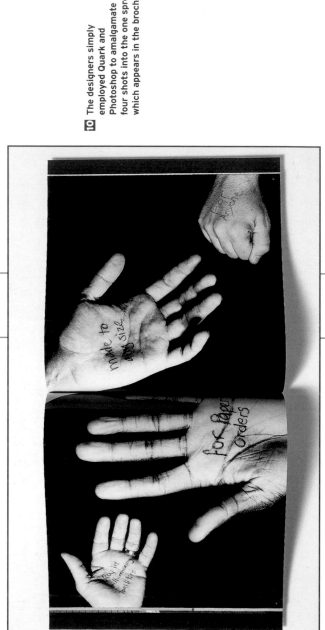

10

DETAILS
Johnson Banks
Studio 6, 92 Lots Road
London
SW10 0QD, UK
tel: +44 171 351 7734
fax: +44 171 351 4435
e-mail: .ohnbank@johnsonbanks.co.uk

HARDWARE/SOFTWARE
Apple Mac 9600 and lots of difficult format cameras,
model-making, embroidery etc.
General layout: QuarkXPress.
Generating visuals: Freehand, Illustrator, Photoshop.
Retouching: Photoshop and Live Picture.

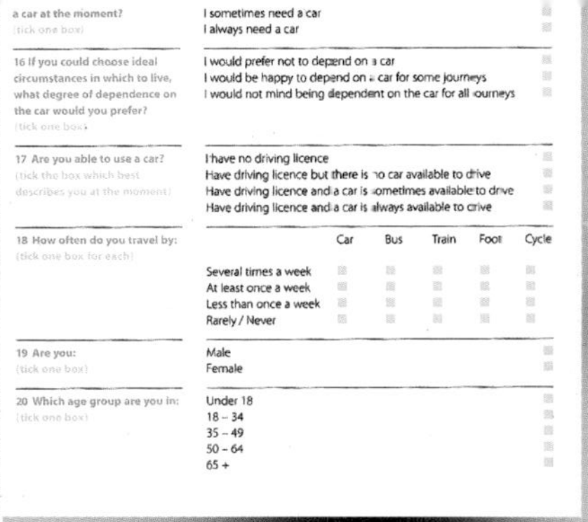

Biography

London multi-disciplinary design consultancy Llewelyn-Davies likes to take on board everything from architecture and planning to health service consultancy and policy recommendation. Its graphic design arm offers an equally eclectic range of services, undertaking work in areas such as public art, corporate literature, identity, signage and publicity. When senior graphic designer Ting Lam Tang joined the company in 1997, he brought with him a string of international prizes and awards, particularly for his typographic work. It's his passion; last year he was an assessor for the prestigious Society of Typographic Designers Awards, for whom he's been a consultant since 1996.

When Ting was brought on board a Llewelyn-Davies project for client Oxfordshire County Council and Cherwell District Council, he was told he had less than four days to produce the job – i.e. go from the initial brief to a completed print run of 10,000. The job in question – a questionnaire intended to investigate travelling habits in and around the county's Banbury region – came from the councils' planning departments via Llewelyn-Davies' planning division. The form's results would contribute to a wider document which would effect a better transport system in the area, with an eye to environmental concerns. The design, production and stock used for the form therefore had to embrace these environmental issues.

'I THINK ORNAMENTATION IN THIS KIND OF DESIGN CAN OFTEN BE CONFUSING. IT'S USUALLY THERE AS NON-FUNCTIONAL DECORATION, AN EYE-CATCHING DEVICE THAT DETRACTS FROM THE INFORMATION YOU'RE TRYING TO IMPART.'

This questionnaire asks for your views on important
good wines in the found, again we found some clue
information on particular things

1

Initial
approach

Ting wasn't fazed by the short lead time: 'I don't believe that it's an excuse for producing substandard work, and if you put your energy into the creative idea then its implementation should be fairly straightforward,' he asserts. 'It's important not to be intimidated by and fixated on the deadline,' he adds. From the beginning, Ting knew he wanted something that was clear, concise and, above all, convenient for the user. 'Lots of designers of this kind of material take the aesthetic point of view as their main criteria; it's a common error.'

'I WAS LUCKY TO BE WORKING WITH A BIG TEAM, BOTH AT THE PLANNING DIVISION OF LLEWELYN-DAVIES AND AT THE CLIENT'S; IT MAKES FOR A SOPHISTICATED APPROACH, ALLOWS MORE VARIED RESPONSES AND OBJECTIVE VIEWPOINTS.'

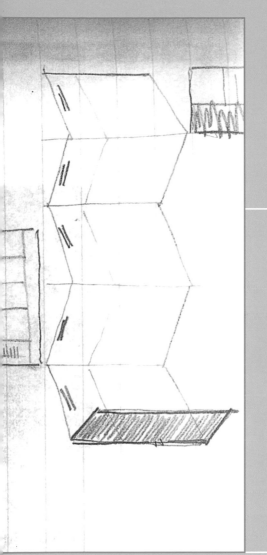

1 The first version Llewelyn-Davies offered the client was an A4 booklet, but when Ting sketched ideas for a second version, he came up with a five-page fold-out concertina which was accepted by the council. 'I think the concertina's more elegant and works better,' says Ting. 'You can see the whole thing too, which I think is important for the user,' he adds.

Ting's decision to use no ornamentation of any kind – logos, illustrations, etc. – was quite a radical one, giving the form a very weighty and professional feel. 'I think ornamentation in this kind of design can often be confusing. It's usually there as non-functional decoration, an eye-catching device that detracts from the information you're trying to impart. It's the same as good advertising, where if you use simple and concise ideas a message will come across far better than if you put too much in there, which simply obscures what you're trying to say,' he believes. Given this lack of visual candy, Ting had to rely instead on strong colour use. He decided on the vibrant green because 'it's contemporary and visually gets across the environmental aspects of the questionnaire.'

'But as people were required to fill in parts of these forms on moving vehicles, the design had to first and foremost deal with ease of use and clarity,' says Ting. Luckily, the client was not one who demanded lots of changes or versions, but even if they had, Ting says any good designer should be able to back up design decisions in a way that's persuasive enough to get their work through – 'you can't blame the client for bad form design, that responsibility lies with the designer!'

Development

Ting believed strongly that as the designer he should have no preconceptions about the project, so took as his starting point the content. Firstly, he realised that there were far too many questions and that these could be pared down and collapsed into a smaller document. 'A form is about users being able to understand what's required and supply the information easily, it shouldn't necessitate too much analysis on their part,' he explains.

His first feeling about the design was that the cover and introduction needed to be laid out as distinct from the rest of the form's content. Reading on, he realised that he needed to design a grid and table which could be easily used. He decided that non-integrated questions in bold colour would effectively distinguish them from the answer sections. For the section heads he began with the idea of simply using a bold, heavier weight of the Myriad font used throughout the form. On implementation, he realised that the text blended in too much with the rest of the document and needed a stronger design solution, so extended the colour to a WOB band, which was then elongated to cover the width of each leaflet page.

2 Ting originally planned to have the section heads in bold green, but on implementation realised that the text blended in too much with the rest of the document. He extended the colour to a WOB band, which was then elongated to cover the width of each leaflet page, as the blue instructions on this sketch illustrate.

3 From the outset Ting knew that the cover and introduction of the form needed to feel different to the rest of the document, so while both use the eight-column grid that features throughout the layout, they are differentiated through the simple use of no text in the first column.

THESE QUESTIONS ARE ABOUT YO

13 How much do you need a car at
I have no need for a car
I sometimes need a car
I always need a car

14 If you could choose ideal circum
degree of dependence on the car wo
I would prefer not to depend on a c
I would be happy to depend on a ca
I would not mind being dependent

15 Are you able to use a car? Tick t
the moment
I have no driving licence
I have a driving licence but there is
I have a driving licence and a car is
I have a driving licence and a car is

16 In what way would you like to c
I would prefer to dispense with my
I would prefer to acquire my own
I am happy to continue as I am

17 Are you: (tick one box)
male
female

18 Which age group are you in: (t
Under 18
18-34
35-49
50-64
65+

PART OF THE
PLEASE COMPLETE THIS QUESTIONNAIRE IS ABOUT
YOUR VIEWS
AND TRAVEL

THESE QUESTIONS ARE ABOUT WORKING AND SHOPPING
IN BANBURY AND EL WHERE

1 Do you work (tick one box)
yes I do not work
(write in number)

2 How often do you visit (tick one box only)
3 or more times a week
1 or 2 times a week
Less than once a week
Less than once a month
Less often / never
Other (write in)
None

3 Where else do you regularly (tick all boxes that apply)
Birmingham
Bicester
Coventry
Warwick
Leamington Spa
Northampton
Oxford
Stratford upon Avon
Other (write in)
None

4 (write in answer)

5 (tick one box only)
Nearest town to my home
Nearest town to my work
Good range and quality of shops
Attractive /pleasant place to go shopping
Easy parking
Free parking /cheap parking
Other (write in)

6 What would encourage you to (tick as many boxes as apply)
More comfortable bus services
Quicker bus services
More or better shops and facilities
Cheaper parking
Easier parking
Less traffic
Better footpaths and pedestrian crossings
Other (write in)

7 Do you expect to visit Banbury (tick one box)
Yes
No
Don't Know

'IT'S CRUCIAL TO SET AN EXAMPLE WHEN WORKING WITH TYPOGRAPHY. MOST OF THE TIME I HAVE TO DO THINGS PROPERLY AND FOLLOW THE RULES SET OUT BY HART'S RULES, BECAUSE I THINK THEY'RE THERE FOR A REASON. SO MY BRACKETS ARE TRACKED BY 10, MY EN RULES AND DASHES ARE TRUE ONES – SOME PEOPLE MIGHT THINK I'M TOO FUSSY, BUT I THINK IT'S IMPORTANT.'

BANBURY TRAVEL SURVEY

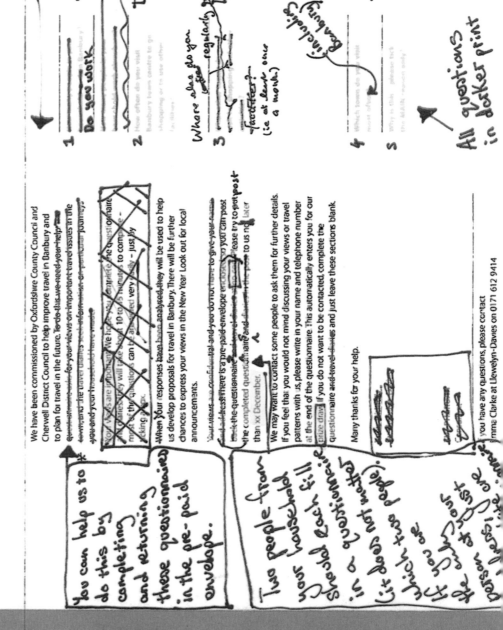

YOU CAN HELP WITH PLANNING TRAVEL TO AND WITHIN BANBURY AND COULD WIN A PRIZE!

We have been commissioned by Oxfordshire County Council and Cherwell District Council to help improve travel in Banbury and to plan for travel in the future.

When your responses have been analysed, they will be used to help us develop proposals for travel in Banbury. There will be further chances to express your views in the New Year. Look out for local announcements.

We may want to contact some people to ask them for further details. If you feel that you would not mind discussing your views or travel patterns with us, please write in your name and telephone number at the end of the questionnaire. This automatically enters you for our prize draw. If you do not want to be contacted, complete the questionnaire and travel diaries and just leave these sections blank.

Many thanks for your help.

Typographic detailing

Ting's decision to use Myriad was based on a number of factors, but uppermost were considerations of legibility and the fact that he'd decided he was going to use one font throughout, which meant it had to have a large family. 'I also wanted something contemporary which would reflect the subject matter,' he says. By using some six weights in the Myriad family, Ting has successfully distinguished sections heads, questions, guidance text and multiple choice answers. Combined with the simple and flexible eight-column grid, the form manages to present a deceptively large amount of information in an uncluttered and concise manner.

Working techniques

Ting always starts the design process on paper before moving on to the Mac, on which he designed the finished form using QuarkXPress: 'Paper allows you to work out the structure and architecture of a job – and it's important because when you visualise something on paper, it's very different to doing the same thing on screen. And also, if you work on screen too much you can end up using the machine as a creative tool, in effect letting the computer and its programs direct the design,' he points out.

Once it came to working with the form's paper, which had to be 100% recycled stock, Ting thought he might hit problems such as show-through and bleed. 'Heavy weights proved prohibitively expensive, so whereas we started with a 250gsm stock we had to go right down to 90gsm to stay within the budget and minimise postal costs for the council,' explains Ting. 'It's not ideal as the optimum would have been a heavier weight, but through constant liaison with the printer we were able to ensure that there was no show-through of the green or ink coming through the page. It worked surprisingly well,' he concludes.

4 The client had originally thought about laying out the questions for the travel diary horizontally along the top of a gridded box in which answers could be entered, but Ting turned this around for greater clarity, creating a clean space which clearly delineates the individual boxes in which to enter answers.

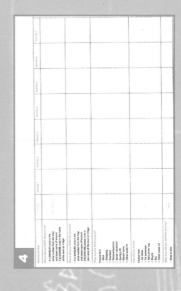

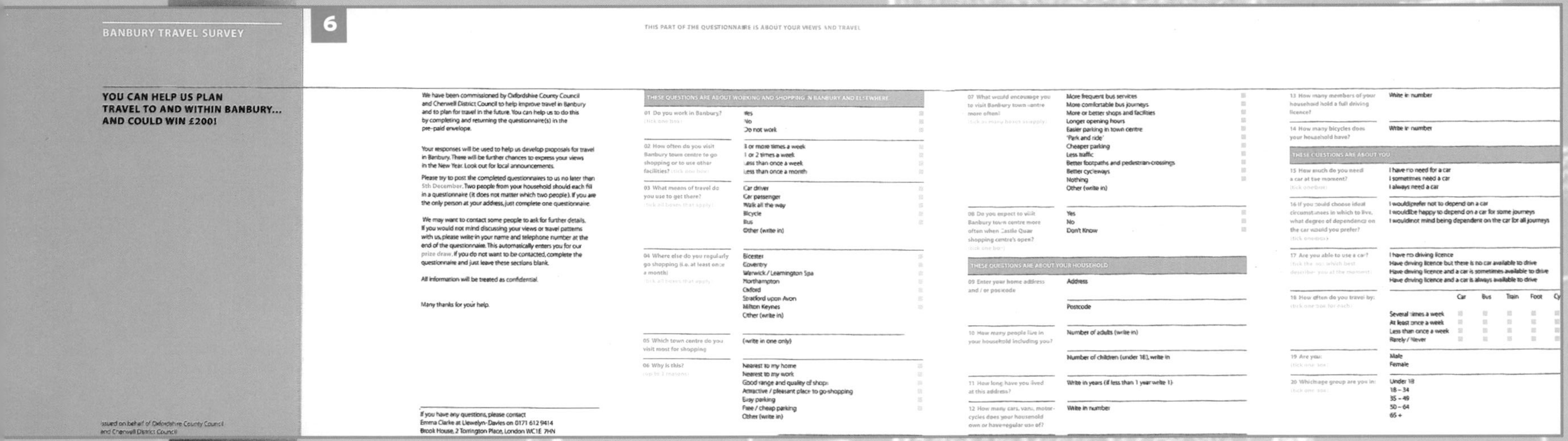

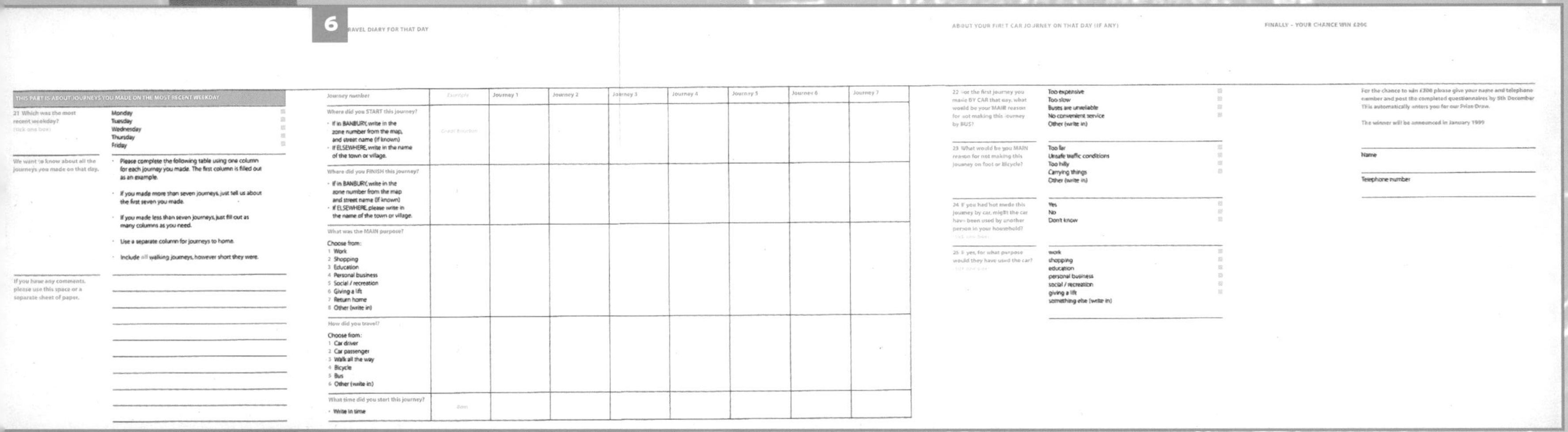

5 The numerous questions the council wanted on the form were pared down and collapsed into a more manageable document, resulting in a much clearer, more uncluttered form which doesn't require too much analysis on the part of the user, something Ting believes is very important in form design.

6 Ting, a keen follower of the typographic rules set out in seminal publications such as *Hart's Rule*, used just one typeface in the design of the form, but was able to deceive the eye through a judicious use of weights and sizes. 'For example, I made the bold coloured questions 0.25pt smaller than the lighter 8pt questions so that they would look the same size. I didn't want to go too small as I wanted it to be about the same size as the most common reading matter, which is newspapers and magazines,' explains Ting. The finished concertina document, both sides of which are shown here, is an easy-to-use, simple form which garners all the information requested by the council without feeling daunting to the user.

DETAILS
Ting Lam Tang
Llewelyn-Davies
Brook House
Torrington Place
London WC1E 7HN
UK
tel: +44 171 637 0181
fax: +44 171 637 8740

SOFTWARE
QuarkXPress 4.0.

'A SENSE OF IRISHNESS IN THE
LOGO WAS ESSENTIAL, BUT NOT
IN CLICHÉD ICONS SUCH AS
HARPS, SHAMROCKS AND THE
COLOUR GREEN,'

Biography

Motion graphics have come a long way from the simple static affairs that involved putting a silver statuette on a rostrum and filming it as it slowly revolved, now they have to amaze and delight audiences while also conveying the brand values of whichever station they're fronting. This shift has been largely due to the innovative design work and canny commissioning of the BBC, which, with its fluffy twos, flocks of twos on a pond, exploding twos and even themed ones and twos for Christmas campaigns featuring Wallis and Gromit, has raised the profile – and the stakes – of the art immeasurably. The BBC has a 50-strong graphic design department at its beck and call, and the kudos, money and clout to commission the likes of Lambie Nairn and Company, regarded by some as the best – and the most expensive in the business. But if you're a new independent Irish TV station looking for an affordable but inventive and imaginative identity package which includes an onscreen logo, logo launch animation sequence, screen stings, a corporate identity, stationery, signage and press packs, to whom do you turn?

The brief and initial approach

TV3, owned by a consortium of Irish investors and CanWest/Global, was in this position last year when it was launched as Ireland's third television station, which would be in direct competition with not only well-established Irish television stations, but also UK terrestrial and European satellite channels. 'The station's target audience was 25-45 year olds, and the company's maxim was one of producing straight-up entertainment with a strong emphasis on news and current affairs programming,' explains Brian Nolan, managing director of Dynamo, the Dublin-based design group which won the three-way pitch for the job. 'The overall feel that was required was one of a fresh, dynamic, young channel with an Irish/European feel – ie. the Irish roots were not to be ignored, but the overall look was to be European,' he adds.

Dynamo, established in 1992 and headed up by Nolan and co-partners Jamie Helly and Brian Williams works in corporate and brand identity development, packaging and motion graphics, so was perfectly suited to the multi-disciplinary task, which may be why it won out over its two English competitors. 'Our pitch was based on an open approach to the brief. The entire creative body of the studio collected as many references and interpretations of the number three that we could find. This resulted in a vast collection of photo stills, video-grabs and found objects, supplemented by our own graphic sketches. These were then edited together in an animated sequence set to the track "Three is the Magic Number". The idea was to demonstrate to the client that there were a thousand ways to interpret the project task,' explains Nolan. Dynamo also presented three test logos applied across the range for onscreen, print and livery – 'to determine the client's preferences for the channel voice and market position. Each logo tackled a different stylistic approach, although each was heavily based upon the numeral 3,' he adds.

1 'All ideas were storyboarded on paper before we even touched the computer,' explains Nolan of this early rough/mood-board and a black-and-white final phase of the roughs for the logo-marque.

1

'IRISH PEOPLE HAVE RECOGNISED AND NOW PLACE A VALUE ON IRISHNESS. THIS FACTOR IS OFTEN INTANGIBLE – A FEEL, A SENSE OF STYLE, A REFLECTION OF THEIR OWN TASTES AND CULTURAL VALUES. IT WAS ESSENTIAL THAT THESE VALUES WERE INCORPORATED INTO THE IDENTITY.'

Development
Dynamo felt strongly that TV3 needed the identity to achieve a number of goals: It had to reflect the ethos and personality of the station. It had to project an entertainment channel in a contemporary and stylish manner. It had to work with the programming and presentation styles. It had to capture the essence of the offer or it would simply have become a corporate marque.

While Dynamo's initial logo presentations tackled various symbol and type combinations; numeral backed up by type, stand-alone number, logotype only etc., the team working on the project felt strongly that the end marque should be a combination of a symbol and the written word, i.e. tvthree. Nolan says it is intended that future developments of the identity will use the symbol alone once public awareness of the station and its marque is greater.

tv▾three

5 From the outset, Dynamo worked around the idea of 'three as the magic number' and devised hundreds of graphic representations and interpretations of the number.

6 Creating a sense of excitement and anticipation with the reverse countdown from one to three.

7 The finished logotype as it appears on screen and throughout the TV3 livery.

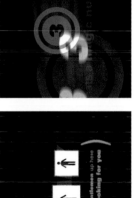

4 The sting was designed to be text-heavy because it had graphic appeal and emphasised the rhythm, humour and quirky nature of the vox-pops.

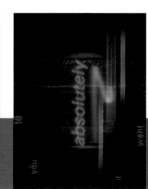

2 The overall theme of the promo is that TV3 is the long-anticipated people's channel. The use of words and graphic symbols to illustrate the speech patterns of the public was done for impact and to add an element of curiosity, humour and anticipation to the station's programming.

3 The copy for the sting is based on vox-pops of Irish people using the number 3. Dynamo recorded various Irish regional accents: 'Most of them were quite natural, some had to be prompted and others were quite bizarre,' says Nolan. 'We had a wide selection of vox-pops which we edited down with regard to accent, content and animation potential,' he adds.

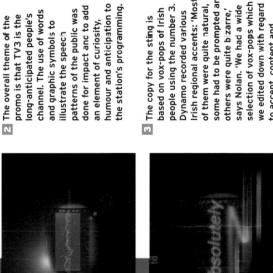

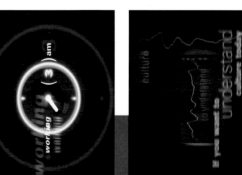

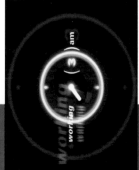

'UNIVERS IS THE VISIBLE AND CONSISTENT VOICE OF TV3, USED ACROSS THE BOARD; ONSCREEN, PRINT AND ADVERTISING. IT HAS A CLEAN AND MODERN FEEL, IS HIGHLY LEGIBLE AND TRANSLATED TO SCREEN WITHOUT ANY DIFFICULTY. ON THE STING, IT OFFERED A SENSE OF RHYTHM TO THE PIECE, AS WELL AS BEING PERFECT FOR ACCENTUATING THE VARIOUS INTONATIONS OF THE VOICES AND ACCENTS.'

Working Process

The group began by paring down the wide variety of ideas which had been used in the original pitch to work up ideas for the initial direction logos. 'For the second presentation, it was back to the drawing-board, with everything as a potential option. The selection was narrowed down to place emphasis on the numeral and our own preference was developed across the range of initial requirements. This was approved, with a few minor tweaks.

The design team consisted of five designers including the project manager, all of whom, in the early stages of development, were involved in both the identity project and the motion graphics. In later stages these was pared down to one or two designers per project. The principals were project manager Jamie Helly, senior designer Paul McBride and Brian Williams on motion graphics.

The group say that the choice of colour as a blue/green (pantone 320) was settled on 'to combine an Irish and European feel around the marque, as well as being a lively contemporary colour that translates from print to TV seamlessly. The tvthree logotype underneath the numeral acts as a foundation and was typeset in Univers light and bold, in order to emphasise the numeral 3 both in the swoosh-shaped symbol and in the logotype itself – three being the magic number.' Much thought was put into the typeface of the sting, and eventually Dynamo decided to go with the Univers used in the onscreen logotype, in order to emphasise the whole TV3 corporate identity programme. The extensive family was used in a variety of weights and sizes – light, regular, bold, black, extra black and oblique.

'This is the visible and consistent voice of TV3, used across the board in all onscreen, print and advertising,' says Dynamo. 'We felt the typeface was very adaptable, and it was available in a large selection of weights, which would offer considerable choice for all the station's applications.

8 The blue/green (pantone 320) colour used throughout the commission was settled on 'to combine an Irish and European feel around the marque, as well as being a lively contemporary colour that translates from print to TV seamlessly,' says Nolan.

9 Dynamo is working up a style guide for the station that will cover all the variants in which the marque may be used, including a white out of black and green out of black marque.

8

It has a clean and modern feel, is highly legible and translates to screen without any difficulty. As regards the sting, it offered a sense of rhythm to the piece, as well as being perfect for accentuating the various intonations of the voices and accents,' enthuses Nolan.

All the TV3 work was executed on the Mac platform. The animation sequence was constructed in Adobe AfterEffects and the editing and sound completed in Media 100. For the promo all ideas were storyboarded on paper before even touching the computer. When it came to animation of the words, the computer applications afforded a certain amount of fluidity to the delivery of the sentences, but a massive amount of work went into the construction of these sentences and images. Ultimately it is a means to an end, a tool which enabled ideas to be realised,' say the group.

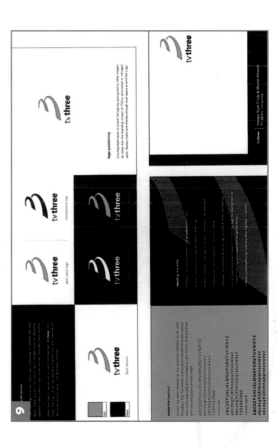

9

Nolan and Dynamo feel that in the TV3 identity, they succeeded in creating something that 'was not simply about maximising return on investment in design, but creating, sustaining and maintaining an image across all the dimensions of the station's broadcasting.' 'Overall it was a dynamic interpretation of the number 3. It had personality, individuality and a certain synergy that we felt was important in representing the new television station,' concludes Nolan. As the sting for TV3's launch won a Promax & BDA Europe Gold Award in the 2D/3D Animation section earlier this year and took a bronze award from ILAD – The Irish Institute of Creative Advertising and Design – Nolan and Dynamo obviously have every right to be proud of the work.

SOFTWARE
Adobe Illustrator, Adobe Photoshop, Adobe AfterEffects, Media 100.

DETAILS
Dynamo Design Consultants
5 Upper Ormond Quay
Dublin 7
Ireland
tel: +353 1 672 9244
fax: +353 1 872 9224
e-mail: triann@dynamo.ie
website: www.dynamo.ie

GALLERY

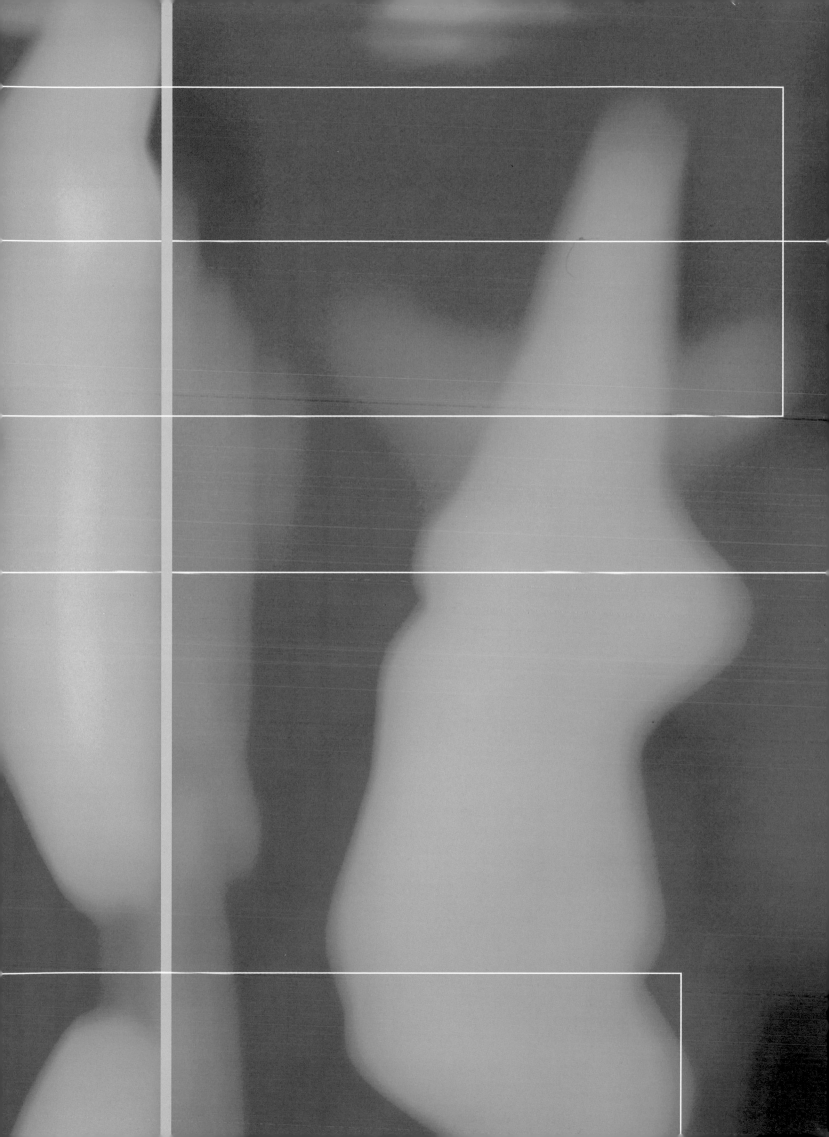

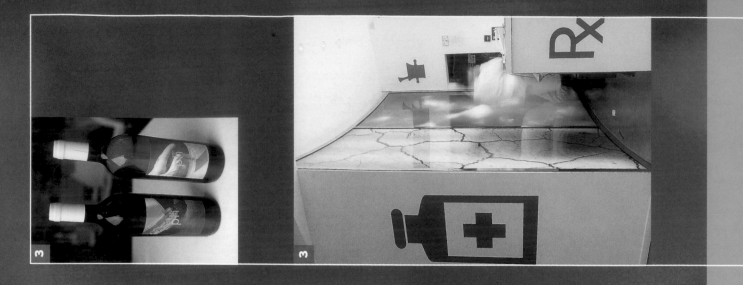

A B C D E F G
A B C D E F G

EXCET

A FONT BASED ON EARLY
GREEK STONECARVING

THIS IS
MASON

INCLUDED in the font are a number of ligatures expressing often used complete words such as 'THE' and 'TO'. ABCDEFGHIJK LMNOPQRSTU VWXY Z R

1 Font catalogue designed by Barnbrook and aimed at promoting his fonts and website at www.virus.com.

2 Fonts designed by Jonathan Barnbrook.

3 Interior panels and wine labels for Damien Hirst's restaurant 'The Pharmacy' in West London.

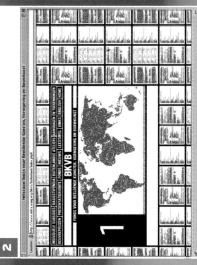

1 Book cover for Kevin Kelly's latest book.

2 Screengrabs of the website for The funding Foundation of Fine Arts, Design and Architecture. 'The design of the site is based on the look and feel of forms and bureaucratic systems.'

3 Intrawebsite for the design and art department of Dutch telecom company KPN. The site gives an insight into the product design output of KPN.

4 *Mediaculture in Europe* was published in Spring 1999 as a sourcebook on new media about art, research, innovation, participation, public domain, learning, education and policy.

LA POSTE

1 TECNIFIBRE

LES PÊCHERIES DE·NOSSI·BÉ

3

ANISETTE

UN CARACTÈRE CRÉÉ PAR JEAN-FRANÇOIS PORCHEZ EN 1996

UN CARACTÈRE À DOUBLE CHASSE ET EN 5 SÉRIES, DU ULTRA-LÉGER AU NOIR

⊕ MÉLANGES · CORPS 60 ⊕

IL IMPORTE QUE L'AFFICHISTE COMMENCE TOUJOURS PAR LE TEXTE & LE CAMPE, AUTANT QUE FAIRE SE PEUT, AU CENTRE DE SA COMPOSITION. C'EST AUTOUR DU TEXTE QUE DOIT TOURNER LE DESSIN ET NON INVERSEMENT

⊕ MÉLANGES · CORPS 30 ⊕

IL IMPORTE QUE L'AFFICHISTE COMMENCE TOUJOURS PAR LE TEXTE & LE CAMPE, AUTANT QUE FAIRE SE PEUT, AU CENTRE

IL IMPORTE QUE L'AFFICHISTE COMMENCE TOUJOURS PAR LE TEXTE & LE CAMPE, AUTANT QUE FAIRE SE PEUT, AU CENTRE

⊕ ÉTROITS & LARGES · CORPS 18 ⊕

IL IMPORTE QUE L'AFFICHISTE COMMENCE TOUJOURS PAR LE TEXTE ET LE CAMPE A
IL IMPORTE QUE L'AFFICHISTE COMMENCE TOUJO

IL IMPORTE QUE L'AFFICHISTE COMMENCE TOUJOURS PAR LE TEXTE ET LE CAMPE A
IL IMPORTE QUE L'AFFICHISTE COMMENCE TOUJ

IL IMPORTE QUE L'AFFICHISTE COMMENCE TOUJOURS PAR LE TEXTE ET LE C
IL IMPORTE QUE L'AFFICHISTE COMMENCE TO

IL IMPORTE QUE L'AFFICHISTE COMMENCE TOUJOURS PAR LE TE
IL IMPORTE QUE L'AFFICHISTE COMMENC

IL IMPORTE QUE L'AFFICHISTE COMMENCE TOUJOURS PAR LE TE
IL IMPORTE QUE L'AFFICHISTE COMMENC

⊕ LES GRAISSES · ULTRA-LÉGER, LÉGER, NORMAL, GRAS, NOIR ⊕

2

Une Incise avec
Angie Sans
Malgré la sensualité des courbes des bas-de-casse
Créé en 1994
un vrai italique
Angie Sans
L'Angie Sans puise ses formes des capitales romaines
par Jean-François Porchez
& un gras
Angie Sans
Deux séries de chiffres : 0123456789 & 0123456789
Angie Sans

1 Logotypes and lettering.

2 Postcard for Angie Sans, 1994.

3 Postcard for Anisette typeface.

34th NEW YORK
34th NEW YORK
FILM FESTIVAL

5

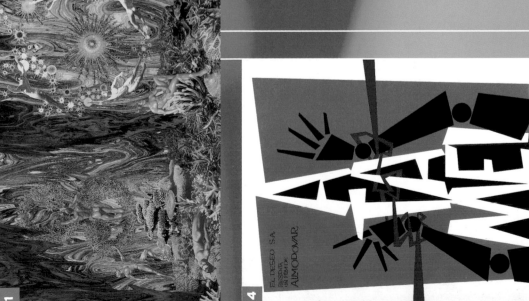

1 Illustration for the magazine *Visionaire*, 'The Alphabet issue'.

2 Fashion photography for Spanish *Vogue* magazine.

3 Graphic material for use in printed and promotional material for Almodóvar's film 'High Heels'.

4 Poster for Almodóvar's film 'Átame'.

5 Typography for the poster for the New York Film Festival.

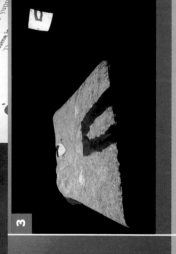

1 Essentially a graphics project, this visual device linked all areas of the museum. Interspersed with interactive screens, it guided visitors round in place of more traditional oriental signage.

2 This HK$10m extravaganza was aimed at schools, employees and corporate visitors. Looking at applications and developments in the world of telecommunications, it included original pieces of commissioned art.

3 The recently re-opened NMPFT in Bradford commissioned MET to design the UK's first ever gallery dedicated to new media. *Blueprint* magazine described the finished work as 'an exciting space full of exhibits which are designed to tease meaning and communicate facts with equal measure.'

4 Science For Life won three major awards and was described by David Attenborough as 'one of the most exciting and innovative exhibitions on science that you will find anywhere in this country'.

1 Some characters from the MoveMe MultipleMaster fonts, 1994.

2 Custom typeface families for Sun Microsystems, 1997.

3 TheSansMonoCondensed, 1997.

4 The family Jesus Loves You all, 1995.

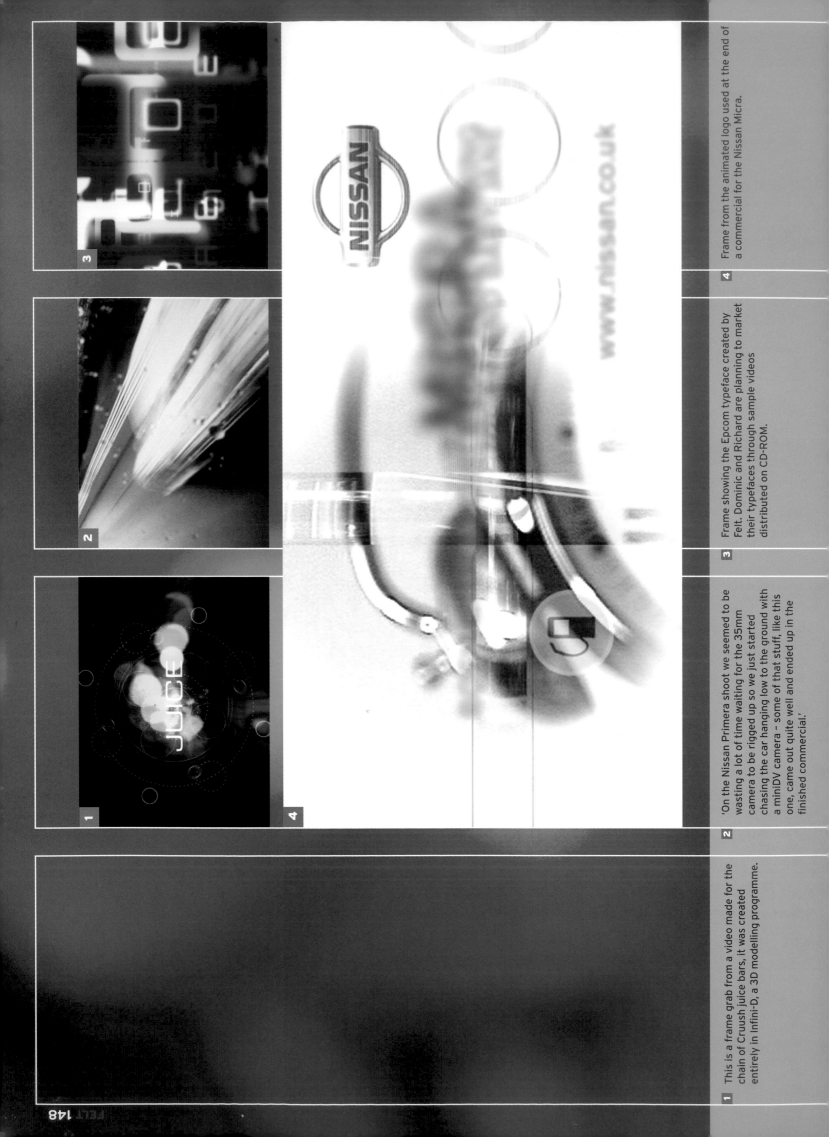

1 This is a frame grab from a video made for the chain of Cruush juice bars, it was created entirely in Infini-D, a 3D modelling programme.

2 'On the Nissan Primera shoot we seemed to be wasting a lot of time waiting for the 35mm camera to be rigged up so we just started chasing the car hanging low to the ground with a miniDV camera – some of that stuff, like this one, came out quite well and ended up in the finished commercial.'

3 Frame showing the Epcom typeface created by Felt. Dominic and Richard are planning to market their typefaces through sample videos distributed on CD-ROM.

4 Frame from the animated logo used at the end of a commercial for the Nissan Micra.

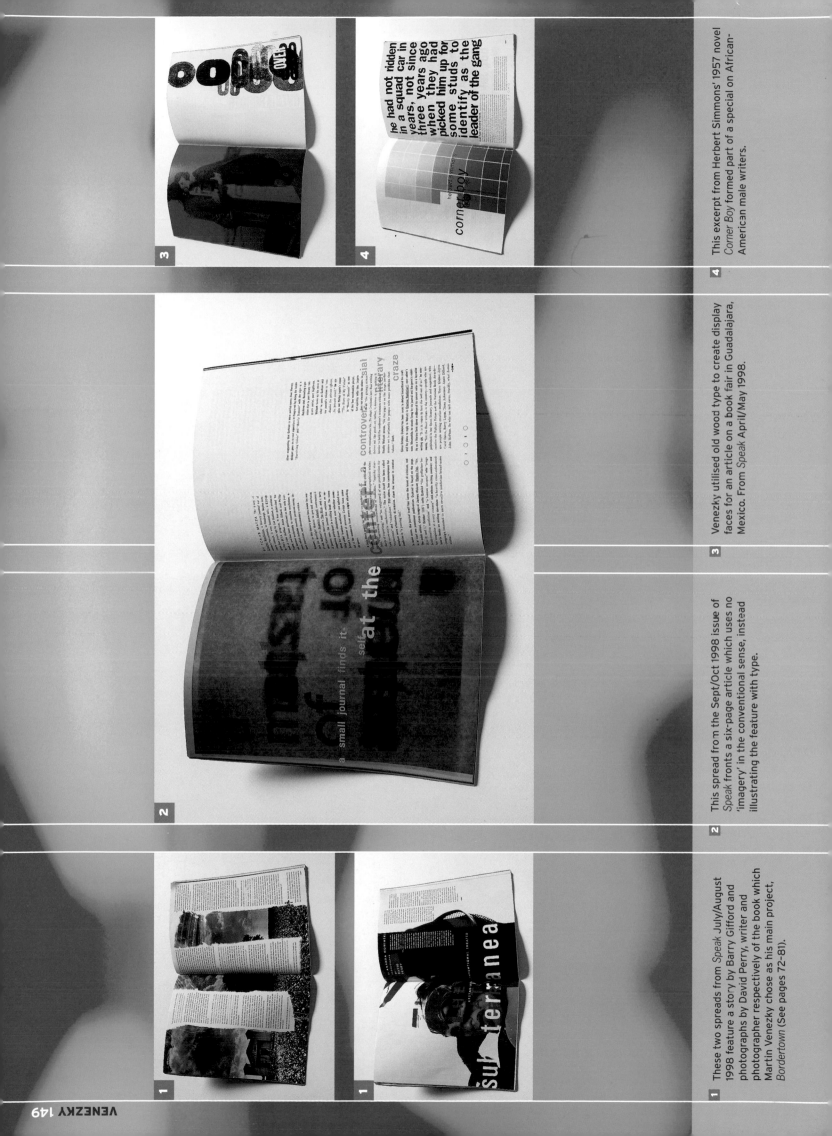

3

4

2

1

1

1 These two spreads from *Speak* July/August 1998 feature a story by Barry Gifford and photographs by David Perry, writer and photographer respectively of the book which Martin Venezky chose as his main project, *Bordertown* (See pages 72–81).

2 This spread from the Sept/Oct 1998 issue of *Speak* fronts a six-page article which uses no 'imagery' in the conventional sense, instead illustrating the feature with type.

3 Venezky utilised old wood type to create display faces for an article on a book fair in Guadalajara, Mexico. From *Speak* April/May 1998.

4 This excerpt from Herbert Simmons' 1957 novel *Corner Boy* formed part of a special on African-American male writers.

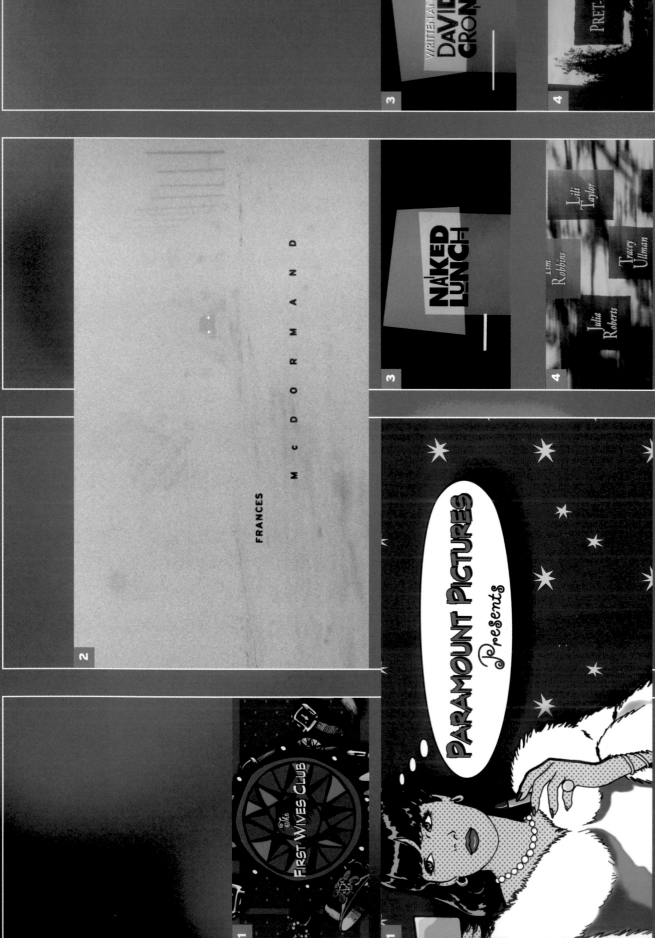

1 'The First Wives Club' (1996)
B&E used a blend of advertising clip art, and pop art inspired backgrounds to give a sense of the unreality of the cultural programming of the early 1960s, when the film begins. Images courtesy of Paramount Pictures.

2 'Fargo' (1995)
The film opens on a wide view of a car snowstorm, barely visible. 'For title lettering, we tried to go with the bleakness of the shot, using very plain highway style lettering (Interstate Bold) as tiny and letterspaced as we could make it and still keep it legible. In this way the lettering seems to be engulfed by the storm, instead of dominating it as a conventional title treatment would have done.' Images courtesy of Gramercy Pictures.

3 'Naked Lunch' (1991)
B&E wanted a content-filled title sequence – Eisenhower, The Bomb, typewriter text, etc. – but found these contents ended up fighting with the film. 'We finally realised that the only solution would be a totally abstract sequence that alluded to the period with shapes and colours. All the lettering is from the Futura family, thoroughly mixed up to create the feeling of a puzzle.'

4 'Preta-Porter' (Ready-to-wear) (1994)
The concept for this structure came from the director, Robert Altman and editor, Geraldine Peroni. 'We added the idea of putting all the credits on pieces of coloured fabric, as the film is all about people in the fashion industry.' Images courtesy of Miramax Films.

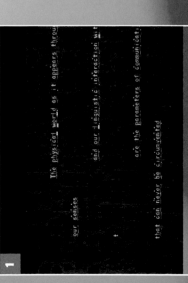

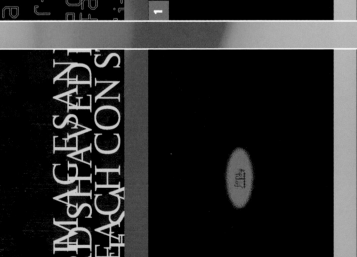

1 The fontBoy screensaver can be downloaded free from the site at www.fontBoy.com/swag – and it's in Mac format only!

2 The fontBoy website acts as a 'digital typeface foundry' that distributes digital typefaces which Aufuldish and others have designed, including roarShock (12C dingbats) typefaces 1–6, Bob Aufuldish:n, 1995.

3 *Purr Porpoise*, proposed book cover, designer/photographer Bob Aufuldish.

4 *The Spiral Dance* book cover, designer/illustrator Kathy Warinner.

5 Study with experimental typeface, Panspermia, designer/photographer Bob Aufuldish.

1 Entertainment company BMG's Asia site.

2 Pages from Lemon's own website at www.lemon.com.hk.

3 This Lemon-designed website formed part of a global event celebrating the opening of a new site for the ZKM Center for Art and Media in Karlsruhe, Germany. The ZKM is dedicated to the relation between art and new media technologies.

1 British Council Stubbs/Hirst poster: Part of a 12 poster set for British Council offices worldwide. The aim was to show how Britain is changing, in this case by substituting half a Stubbs horse with a Damien Hirst sheep in formaldehyde.

2 V&A spiral mailer: designed to influence public opinion about the proposed extension to the V&A designed by Daniel Libeskind. An enclosing box falls apart to reveal a paper model of the building.

3 Mecklenburgh Opera corporate identity: the 'staged' type reflects the company's contemporary work in modern music theatre.

4 One of a set of 42 classroom cards designed to be used within the 900 classrooms worldwide in which the British Council teaches English. This one deals with comparative superlatives.

5 Advertising/design lecture poster: A Michael Johnson talk about the similarities between advertising and design: "I was looking at the word "advertising" and design: "I was looking at the word "advertising" and realised that if I put an "N" on the end of it, I could make the word "design" out of it", says Johnson.

THERE'S NOT MUCH DIFFERENCE BETWEEN ADVERTISING AND DESIGN. A TALK BY MICHAEL JOHNSON, JOHNSON BANKS

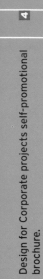

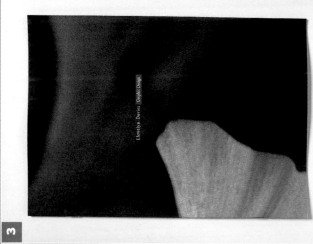

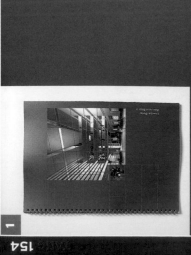

1 Design for Healthcare projects self-promotional brochure.

2 Corporate brochure for McBains Construction Consultants.

3 Design for Corporate projects self-promotional brochure.

4 Brochure for Riverbank House Team.

1 Irish computer company IONA technologies' conference signage from 1999, and a still from the 1998 animation sequence for the company.

2 Identity for film facility house concentrating on high-end digital animation and post-production. Stationery, signage and packaging formed part of the job.

3 Station logo and opticals for Irish TV station TnaG.

4 A still from one of three 30-second TV ads produced for Coca-Cola via ad agency McCann Erickson Puerto Rico.

COLLATING THE TEXT AND IMAGES FOR THIS BOOK ESSENTIALLY INVOLVED MY HARASSING, HARANGUING AND AT TIMES EVEN STALKING DESIGNERS AROUND THE GLOBE – USUALLY VIA THE INTERNET, BUT LONDON TRANSPORT CAME IN USEFUL TOO. EVERYONE INVOLVED IN WHAT WAS A HUGELY COLLABORATIVE UNDERTAKING TOOK IT WITH GOOD GRACE, PATIENCE AND AN EXTRAORDINARY WILLINGNESS TO OPEN UP THEMSELVES, THEIR WORK AND THEIR CREATIVE IDEAS AND SOLUTIONS. I'M HUGELY INDEBTED TO ALL THE DESIGNERS GATHERED TOGETHER HERE FOR THAT AND FOR THE WAY THEY WORKED TO EXPRESS THAT CREATIVITY CLEARLY, BUT OWE THANKS TOO TO LIZ BAILEY, WHO WROTE THE CHAPTERS ON BOB AUFULDISH AND LUC(AS) DE GROOT, AND JOHN CRANMER, WHO DID THE SAME FOR THE FELT AND FRIEZE CHAPTERS. NATALIA PRICE-CABRERA AT ROTOVISION REMAINED CALM, COOL AND COLLECTED IN THE FACE OF MOUNTING PRESSURE, AND MUST BE THANKED FOR HER SUPPORT THROUGHOUT, AS MUST LUCIE PENN AT DESIGN REVOLUTION, WHO WADED THROUGH THE PACKAGES OF DISCS, PAPER AND TRANSPARENCIES TO PULL ALL THESE DIVERSE PROJECTS TOGETHER INTO A COHESIVE DESIGN. PAUL MURPHY AND CHRIS FOGES WERE BOTH EXTREMELY HELPFUL AND INSTRUCTIVE, AND ONCE AGAIN I AM INDEBTED [TO THE B]IT FOUNDATION.